The Baseball Entertainer
#2

The BASEBALL Entertainer #2

EDITED BY

Robert Kuenster

Ivan R. Dee

www.ivanrdee.com

Portions of this book first appeared in *Baseball Digest* magazine.

Library of Congress Control Number:

ISBN-13: 978-1-56663-863-0 (paper)
ISBN-10: 1-56663-863-1 (paper)

PREFACE

When *The Baseball Entertainer*, inaugural edition, appeared in the spring of 2009, it was greeted with huzzahs—and a few catcalls—from the fans. "Too easy!" some screamed. "Too hard," others whined. You can't please everyone, and surely not fans of the Great American Pastime.

But the overall response to that first book of baseball entertainment was so great that we couldn't resist putting together . . . *Son of Baseball Entertainer*, or *The Return of Baseball Entertainer*, as some pundits suggested. Instead we decided to keep it simple: *The Baseball Entertainer #2*. It's all completely new, a fabulous compendium of quizzes, rules challenges, photo games, crossword puzzles, fascinating statistics, and humorous anecdotes, all designed for enjoyment at any hour, anywhere, in the midst of the season or in the chillier months of the Hot Stove League. Many of the answers in this book will surprise you, and some will simply astonish you.

According to Casey Stengel, "There's three things you can do in a baseball game: you can win or you can lose or it can rain." In any eventuality, *The Baseball Entertainer #2* will make good company. Enjoy!

The Baseball Entertainer
#2

QUIZ 1

Answers on page 58

Here are quizzes to test your knowledge of baseball history and its players. Collect ten points for each question answered correctly. (If you score 80 or better, you are a Hall of Fame trivia buff; 70 or better, an MVP performer; 60 to 70, an All-Star; 40 to 60, a minor leaguer.)

Monthly Records

1. Who holds the record for most hits in one month with 68: Ichiro Suzuki, Ty Cobb, Tris Speaker, or Pete Rose?

2. The record for most saves in one month is 15, a feat accomplished by three different closers. Lee Smith was the first to save 15 games in one month when he did it in June 1993 with the St. Louis Cardinals. Chad Cordero did it in June 2005 with the Washington Nationals. Who is the other reliever to save 15 games in one month: Bruce Sutter, John Wetteland, Trevor Hoffman, or Jeff Reardon?

3. The most runs batted in during one month, since 1900, is 53 by Hack Wilson of the Cubs in August 1930 and by what other Hall of Famer: Ted Williams, Chuck Klein, Joe DiMaggio, or Hank Greenberg?

4. Sammy Sosa holds the record for most homers hit in one month with 20 in June 1998 with the Cubs. The previous mark was 18 held by what slugger: Babe Ruth, Rudy York, Albert Belle, or Roger Maris?

5. Since 1900, the most wins by a pitcher in a single month is 10 set by what pitcher in July 1902: Rube Waddell, Christy Mathewson, Walter Johnson, or Cy Young?

6. In 1938 the New York Yankees set an American League record by winning 28 games in the month of August, finishing with a 28-8 mark. The National League record for victories in a month is 29 set by what club in September 1916: Pirates, Cubs, Phillies, or Giants?

7. Since 1900, the most stolen bases in one month is 33 held by which player: Lou Brock, Rickey Henderson, Maury Wills, or Tim Raines?

8. Which one of the following pitchers never tossed five complete-game shutouts in one month: Bob Gibson, Sandy Koufax, Don Drysdale, or Orel Hershiser?

9. Who is the only pitcher to throw two no-hitters in one month of a season: Virgil Trucks, Nolan Ryan, Allie Reynolds, or Johnny Vander Meer?

10. What pitcher holds the record for most strikeouts in one month with 87: Randy Johnson, Nolan Ryan, Pedro Martinez, or Curt Schilling?

CROSSWORD PUZZLE 1

Answer on page 58

ACROSS

1 Pitchers use ____ ____ to keep their hands dry (2wds.)
6 The 1919 Chicago White Sox became known as the ____ Sox after conspiring with gamblers
9 A ____-____ double is a two-base hit that doesn't require a slide
10 Shane Victorino of the Philadelphia Phillies led the majors with 13 in 2009
11 A starting pitcher often ____ his arm after a game
12 Home of the Nationals
14 Scores a lot of runs in an inning
15 Outfielder Juan ____ had 200-hit seasons with the Rockies, Marlins, and Cubs
18 ____ Bennett was a reliever for the Montreal Expos (1997–1999)

20 The 2009 World Series extended into this month
23 He clubbed 34 homers for Tampa Bay in 2003 and 32 for Baltimore in 2008
24 An ____ win usually means a team was lucky to gain a victory
26 Many hits or runs in close succession
27 Teams travel on ____ days
28 The warning ____ tells an outfielder he's near the wall
29 Mickey ____ was a catcher with the A's, Orioles, Tigers, and Rangers (1984–1997)

DOWN

1 A player who's been inactive is likely to show some ____ when he returns
2 A manager may ____ ____

(2 wds.) his lineup when things are going badly

3 Signals with the head

4 Protested a call on the field

5 Get on base to start an inning: _____ _____ table (2wds.)

6 Outfielder who averaged 37 homers per season with the Pirates, 1999–2002

7 St. Louis was the venue for the 2009 ___-___ Game

8 Pirates reliever Bruce _____ _____ was the winning pitcher in the first World Series night game in 1971

13 He was the longtime owner and manager of the Philadelphia Athletics

16 Cy Young winner for the 1959 White Sox

17 A hard-fought game

19 This Canadian province once had a couple of Pacific Coast League teams

21 Slang for a home run (2 wds.)

22 A long-ball _____ is a player who can homer at any time

23 Turn at the plate (2 wds.)

25 Joe DiMaggio was of _____ (abbr.) descent

THEY SAID IT . . . "I could never play in New York. The first time I came into a game there, I got into the bullpen car and they told me to lock the doors."

—*Mike Flanagan, former Orioles pitcher*

QUIZ 2

Answers on page 60

Home Run Champions

1. There are seven players who have won five or more league home run titles since 1900. Collect ten points if you can identify five of these seven sluggers.

2. Four players with the last name "Williams" have won a league home run crown. Name three of these four players to collect ten points.

3. Three players have captured HR titles in both the American League and National League, with Sam Crawford and Mark McGwire being two. Who is the other: Sammy Sosa, Fred McGriff, Ken Griffey, Jr., or Jim Thome?

4. Which of the following sluggers did not win an N.L. home run crown with the New York Mets: Darryl Strawberry, Howard Johnson, Mike Piazza, or Dave Kingman?

5. What second baseman never led his league in home runs: Bobby Grich, Ryne Sandberg, Rogers Hornsby, or Jeff Kent?

6. Through 2009 there were five switch-hitters who had won a league home run title. Collect two points for each of these players you can identify.

7. Who was the last National League player to win three consecutive home run crowns: Mike Schmidt, Barry Bonds, Mark McGwire, or Ryan Howard?

8. Through 2009, Dick Allen is one of only two Chicago White Sox players to win a league home run title. Who is the other White Sox slugger to accomplish this feat: Frank Thomas, Bill Melton, Harold Baines, or Ron Kittle?

9. The Boston Red Sox have had 13 different league home run champions from 1901 through 2009. If you can name seven of these title winners, collect ten points.

10. True or False. Despite 569 career homers, Rafael Palmeiro never led the league in home runs during his career.

Home Run Fact: *Sammy Sosa holds the mark for most home runs in a season without hitting a grand slam: 63 in 1999.*

Following are ten True or False questions. If you get all ten correct in a given quiz, you are an expert on rules. A score of six to eight correct answers gives you a passing grade. Anything less indicates you need a course in Baseball Rules 101.

Answers on page 62

BASEBALL BY THE RULES
1

1. Melvin Mora of the Rockies hits a fly ball near the third base coaching box. The Rockies' third base coach, in an attempt to avoid Cubs' third baseman Aramis Ramirez, makes contact with Ramirez, who is unable to reach the ball. Coach's interference should be called on the third base coach even though he attempted to avoid making contact with Ramirez.

2. The Dodgers' Matt Kemp hits a pop fly near the first base coach's box. Cardinals' first baseman Albert Pujols tries to position himself to make the catch. The Dodgers' first base coach decides to remain stationary; Pujols runs into him and is unable to make the catch. No interference should be called since the coach has the right to remain in the coach's box at all times.

3. Red Sox pitcher Jon Lester attempts to pick off the Indians' Grady Sizemore at first base. The ball trickles by first baseman Kevin Youkilis. Sizemore is standing on first when the first base coach picks up the ball and hands it to Youkilis. The coach has interfered with the play, but since there's no play being made, the umpire should simply call "Time" and kill the play.

4. The Twins have Denard Span on first and no outs when Joe Mauer hits a ground ball to Tigers third baseman Brandon Inge that looks like a sure double play. To avoid the DP, the Twins' third base coach interferes with Inge. In this case both Span and Mauer should be called out.

5. Braves' pitcher Tim Hudson is in the set position with the Diamondbacks' Justin Upton on first base. As Hudson starts his delivery, the D'Backs third base coach yells "Time" and causes Hudson to balk. The umps allow the balk, reasoning that a major league pitcher should never stop his windup when an opposing coach calls "Time."

6. The Mariners have Ichiro Suzuki on third and Ken Griffey, Jr., on first and one out when Chone Figgins lofts a pop fly to Rays' first baseman Carlos Pena. Griffey is going with the pitch. Pena is positioned under the ball and about to catch it when Figgins crashes into him to break up a potential double play. Because Figgins intentionally interferes to keep the Rays from doubling-up Griffey, the umpires should call Figgins out for interference, and should also call Ichiro out.

7. Mark Teixeira of the Yankees fouls off a Scott Feldman pitch and is called out by the umpire because he had his back foot outside the batter's box. The umpire should not have called Teixeira out because the ball was foul.

8. The Angels have Bobby Abreu on first base and two outs when Hideki Matsui hits an inside-the-park home run and is called "safe" on a close play at the plate. Abreu, however, fails to touch home plate on his trip around the bases. Royals' catcher John Buck appeals that Abreu missed the plate, and Abreu is called out. Matsui's run should not count.

9. The Cubs' Derrek Lee is batting with a count of two balls and two strikes. On the next pitch Lee foul-tips the ball that goes directly into the chest protector of Braves' catcher Brian McCann, who smothers the ball. Lee should be called out on strikes.

10. Dexter Fowler of the Rockies is attempting to steal second base. As Phillies' catcher Carlos Ruiz cocks his arm to throw to second, he accidentally strikes umpire Jim Joyce in the mask. Ruiz hesitates and throws late to second base. Since the umpire is normally considered to be part of the playing field, Fowler should be given a stolen base on the play.

Rule Fact: When attempting the "hidden ball trick," the defensive team's pitcher cannot be on or astride the rubber or he will be called for a balk.

QUIZ 3

Answers on page 63

Decade Leaders 2000–2009

1. Who hit the most home runs in the 2000s (2000–2009) with 435: Barry Bonds, Manny Ramirez, Albert Pujols, or Alex Rodriguez?

2. Which player collected the most base hits in the majors from 2000 through 2009 with 2,030: Derek Jeter, Ichiro Suzuki, Michael Young, or Todd Helton?

3. What pitcher won the most games during the 2000s with 148: Randy Johnson, Curt Schilling, Andy Pettitte, or Greg Maddux?

4. Four different pitchers saved 50 or more games in a single season during the decade, but what closer is credited with the most saves in the 2000s with 397: Trevor Hoffman, Mariano Rivera, Billy Wagner, Francisco Rodriguez, or Roberto Hernandez?

5. Who paced all major league batters with 95 triples during the decade: Jimmy Rollins, Johnny Damon, Carl Crawford, or Juan Pierre?

6. What batter finished the decade with the highest batting average (minimum 4,000 plate appearances) with a .334 mark: Ichiro Suzuki, Todd Helton, Albert Pujols, or Matt Holliday?

7. During the 1970s, Jim Palmer of the Baltimore Orioles tossed the most shutouts (44) during the decade. From 2000 to 2009, what pitcher completed the most scoreless games with 14: Roy Halladay, Tom Glavine, Johan Santana, or Roger Clemens?

8. What team won the most regular-season games during the 2000s with 965: St. Louis Cardinals, New York Yankees, Boston Red Sox, Los Angeles Angels, or Atlanta Braves?

9. Who was the only pitcher to toss two no-hitters during the decade: Randy Johnson, Pedro Martinez, Jon Lester, or Mark Buehrle?

10. Which manager won the most games during the decade with 952 victories: Bobby Cox, Tony La Russa, Joe Torre, or Mike Scioscia?

PHOTO QUIZ 1 *Answers on page 64*

Here is a photo quiz to test your memory of who's who in baseball history. (If you score 80 or better, your memory is excellent; 70 or better, good; 40 to 60, it's slipping.)

1. Collect 10 points for each of these Hall of Famers you can identify. They both won N.L home run titles in the 1950s.

2. Collect 10 points if you can identify this 1959 American League home run champ.

3. Los Angeles Dodgers infielders who played together from 1973 through the 1981 season. Collect 10 points for each player you identify correctly.

4. After these two pitched, Braves fans prayed for rain. Collect 10 points for each player you identify.

5. Collect 10 points if you identify this well-known pitching coach.

Fill in the Blank

Answers on page 66

Here is a quiz challenging you to add the missing player from the list.

1. These clubs had a trio of 40-home run hitters in the year listed. Fill in the missing player who hit 40 or more home runs.

1973 Atlanta Braves: Hank Aaron (40), Darrell Evans (41), and _____ (43).
1996 Colorado Rockies: Andres Galarraga (47), Vinny Castilla (40), and _____ (40).
1997 Colorado Rockies: Andres Galarraga (41), Vinny Castilla (40), and _____ (49).

2. In the 1981 strike-interrupted season, four players tied for the American League lead in home runs with 22. How many of these players can you identify?

_____, Oakland A's
_____, Baltimore Orioles
_____, California Angels
_____, Boston Red Sox

3. From 1968 through 2009, ten pitchers won 25 or more games in a season. How many of these players can you identify?

Year	Wins	Pitcher, Team
1968	31	_____, Detroit Tigers
	26	_____, San Francisco Giants
1969	25	_____, New York Mets
1971	25	_____, Detroit Tigers
1972	27	_____, Philadelphia Phillies
1974	25	_____, Oakland A's
	25	_____, Texas Rangers
1978	25	_____, New York Yankees
1980	25	_____, Baltimore Orioles
1990	27	_____, Oakland A's

QUIZ 4

Answers on page 67

Cy Young Award Winners

1. Who was the youngest pitcher to win the Cy Young Award: Dwight Gooden, Bret Saberhagen, Fernando Valenzuela, or Tim Lincecum?

2. Through 2009, who was the only pitcher to win a Cy Young Award as a 40-year old: Gaylord Perry, Early Wynn, Warren Spahn, or Roger Clemens?

3. Nine pitchers have won a league Most Valuable Player Award and a Cy Young Award in the same season. Collect ten points if you can identify six of these players.

4. Who is the only pitcher to win the Cy Young Award the same season in which he pitched a perfect game: Jim Hunter, Jim Bunning, Sandy Koufax, or Randy Johnson?

5. The Toronto Blue Jays have had three different pitchers capture the Cy Young Award. Collect ten points if you can identify two of these three pitchers.

6. In 1963, 1965, and 1966, Sandy Koufax won the Cy Young Award while striking out 300 or more batters in a season. Five other pitchers have won a Cy Young Award and fanned 300-plus batters in the same season. Collect two points for each of these pitchers you can name.

7. Who was the first relief pitcher to win the Cy Young Award: Rollie Fingers, Mike Marshall, Sparky Lyle, or Bruce Sutter?

8. From 1967 through 1976, the American League had four different pitchers with the first name "Jim" who captured Cy Young honors. Collect ten points if you can identify three of these four hurlers.

9. Who was the first Cy Young Award winner to capture the honor without winning 20 games: Tom Seaver, Dean Chance, Whitey Ford, or Vern Law?

10. Through 2009 there were 15 pitchers who won multiple Cy Young Awards. Collect ten points if you can identify eight of these pitchers.

CROSSWORD PUZZLE 2

Answer on page 68

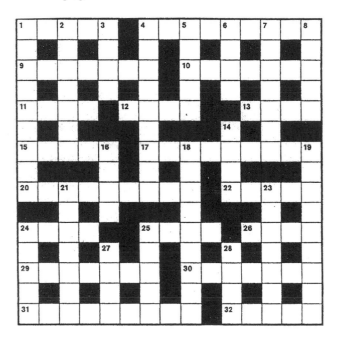

ACROSS

1 Phillies Hall of Fame pitcher _____ Roberts

4 Paul Waner was known as "___ ____" (2 wds.)

9 A smart manager will ____ ___ percentages (2wds.)

10 Ozzie once played shortstop for the White Sox

11 Dusty Baker managed this club in 2009

12 Joint susceptible to injury

13 Left-hander Cliff Lee led the American League with 22 in 2008

15 Banks, who was N.L. MVP in 1958 and 1959

17 Hard to believe, but he was N.L. MVP just once, in 1957

20 Rankings of teams in a division or league

22 A _____ man tries to hold the lead before giving way to the closer

24 The major leagues are often called "the ____"

25 To advance a runner is to ____ him up one or more bases

26 Jorge _____ was an A.L. All-Star second baseman with the White Sox in 1975
29 Hank Aaron Drive is in this city
30 To really connect is to ___ ___ a pitch (2wds.)
31 The Cubs are Chicago's ___ ___ team (2wds.)
32 Touch home plate for a run

DOWN
1 Scribes who cover baseball
2 Inge who plays for the Tigers
3 Nickname of the Washington club
4 Roger _____ was a legendary catcher who introduced the shin guard
5 Eric ___ was the N.L. Cy Young Award winner in 2003
6 One of the Concepcions. He played for the Royals in the 1980s

7 Hall of Fame pitcher Warren Spahn was a decorated _____ during World War II
8 Baseball teams
14 A.L. team that came up short of a world championship in 2008
16 Finishes
18 Home of the Sounds of the Pacific Coast League
19 Hall of Famer who was the A.L.'s first Triple Crown winner back in 1901
21 Lanky
23 The only non-U.S. major league city
24 Ryan _____, slugging outfielder for the Brewers
25 Where the Marlins are based
27 Take a very short lead, _____ off the bag
28 A batted ball that just gets through is said to have "_____ on it"

Name That Hall of Famer

A. My uniform number was 19, and in each of my six 20-win seasons I led my league in victories. I also topped the league in ERA once, shutouts four times, innings pitched five times, and strikeouts seven times. I struck out 15 batters in my first major league start. Who am I?

B. I won league fielding titles as a shortstop and as a center fielder. I was a two-time American League MVP and played my entire career with one team. I finished my career with 3,142 hits. Who am I?

Answers on page 69

QUIZ 5

Answers on page 69

50-Home Run Hitters

1. Through 2009, nine players have had multiple 50-home run seasons. Collect ten points if you can identify six of these players.

2. After Babe Ruth became the first player to reach the 50-homer plateau in a single season, who was the second major league player to accomplish the feat: Jimmie Foxx, Hank Greenberg, Hack Wilson, or Lou Gehrig?

3. Cecil and Prince Fielder are the only father and son major leaguers to hit 50 homers in a season. What pitcher did they both homer against during their 50-home run campaign: Tom Gordon, Roger Clemens, Randy Johnson, Jamie Moyer, or Mike Jackson?

4. Who was the oldest big league player to hit 50 homers in as season: Willie Mays, Barry Bonds, Mark McGwire, or Johnny Mize?

5. Through 2009, only three players had a 50-homer season with two different teams. Collect ten points if you can identify two of these three sluggers.

6. Only three players have hit 50 homers in a season with a slugging percentage below .600. Who registered the lowest slugging percentage (.575) while clubbing 50-plus homers: Cecil Fielder, Ken Griffey, Jr., Brady Anderson, or Andruw Jones?

7. What player was the fastest to reach 50 home runs in a season: Mark McGwire, Roger Maris, Barry Bonds, or Sammy Sosa?

8. Jimmie Foxx was the first player to win a league batting title the same season he clubbed 50 homers. Who is the only other player to achieve this feat: Babe Ruth, Mickey Mantle, Willie Mays, or Johnny Mize?

9. Mark McGwire is one of two players to hit 50 homers in a season and fail to score 100 runs. Who is the other: Andruw Jones, Ralph Kiner, Jim Thome, or David Ortiz?

10. Two Cleveland Indians players have slugged 50 homers in a season. Collect five points for each one you can name.

BASEBALL BY THE RULES

2

Answers on page 71

1. If a fielder has secure possession of the ball but drops it after making immediate contact with the ground or wall, he should get credit for the catch. True or False?

2. If a fielder drops the ball while in the act of transferring it after he has had control and secure possession of the ball, he should get credit for the catch. True or False?

3. If a batted ball strikes the outfielder's glove and goes over the fence in fair territory, the batter should be awarded two bases. True or False?

4. If a batted ball caroms off the body of one fielder and is caught by another fielder, this should be ruled a legal catch as long as the ball doesn't touch the ground, an umpire, a wall, or some object other than the fielder. True or False?

5. If two fielders collide and fall unconscious to the ground, and one fielder has the ball, the catch is not legal until a teammate removes the ball from the fallen player's glove. True or False?

6. If a bouncing batted ball becomes lodged in the webbing of the pitcher's glove, and the pitcher throws the glove *and* the ball to the first baseman to attempt a putout, the first baseman should get credit for a legal catch and the batter-runner should be called out if the ball and glove are caught by the first baseman before the batter-runner reaches first base. True or False?

7. The pitcher fields a slow roller and tosses the ball to the first baseman, who smothers the ball in his armpit for three seconds. This should be ruled a legal catch of a thrown ball, and the batter-runner should be called out since the first baseman had the ball against his body for at least three seconds. True or False?

8. If a fielder catches a batted fly ball and his momentum carries him into the dugout, the catch should be allowed even

22

if he receives assistance from anyone in the dugout to prevent him from falling. True or False?

9. A fielder is allowed to make a catch, carry the ball into the dugout, and make a throw from the dugout as long as he remains on his feet. True or False?

10. If a fielder makes a throw from the dugout and the ball slips out of his hand and drops to the floor of the dugout while he is making the throw, all runners should be awarded two bases from their base position at the start of play. True or False?

11. When catcher's interference is called, the ball should be ruled dead immediately and the batter-runner and all runners awarded one base. True or False?

12. If an outfielder makes a catch and falls into the stands, the ball is ruled dead and all runners are awarded two bases. True or False?

13. When the Infield Fly Rule is called, the ball should be ruled dead immediately to protect the runners. If the fielder drops the ball, the runners should not be allowed to advance. True or False?

14. The Infield Fly Rule can be called only on batted balls that are caught by an infielder. True or False?

15. With runners on first and second and less than two outs, the batter bunts the ball 40 feet in the air to the pitcher. Because the ball was bunted higher than 10 feet, the Infield Fly Rule should be called. True or False?

THEY SAID IT . . .

"The way a team plays as a whole determines its success. You may have the greatest bunch of individual stars in the world, but if they don't play together, the club won't be worth a dime." —*Babe Ruth*

"One of the beautiful things about baseball is that every once in a while you come into a situation where you want to, and where you have to, reach down and prove something." —*Nolan Ryan*

"Show me a good sportsman and I'll show you a player I'm looking to trade." —*Leo Durocher*

QUIZ 6

Answers on page 72

20-Game Winners

1. Over a span of 93 baseball seasons (1917–2009), only two pitchers have won 20 and lost 20 games in the same season. Collect ten points if you can name either of these pitchers. A clue: both pitchers did it during the 1970s.

2. Who posted the highest ERA (5.08) for a 20-game winner: Rick Helling, Jack Morris, Ray Kremer, or Bobo Newsom?

3. What 20-game winner holds the mark for highest winning percentage (.893): Preacher Roe, Ron Guidry, Roger Clemens, or David Cone?

4. Since 1900, Christy Mathewson set the mark with 13 seasons of 20 or more wins. Who is the only other big league pitcher to register 20-plus victories in 13 seasons: Walter Johnson, Grover Alexander, Warren Spahn, or Lefty Grove?

5. Who holds the record for most consecutive 20-win seasons in baseball history with 12: Cy Young, Christy Mathewson, Joe McGinnity, or Mordecai Brown?

6. Four pitchers since 1900 have won 20 or more games in one season for three different teams. Collect ten points if you can identify two of these four hurlers.

7. Since 1958 when they moved to Los Angeles and through 2009, the Dodgers have had 11 different 20-game winners. Claude Osteen accomplished the feat for LA in 1969 and 1972. Collect one point for each of the other ten 20-game winners the Dodgers have had while playing in Los Angeles during that span.

8. True or False: David Cone is the only pitcher to record a 20-win season with both the New York Mets and the New York Yankees.

9. Who is the only pitcher to win 20 games in a season while pitching for two teams and capture the Cy Young Award: Tom Seaver, Rick Sutcliffe, Bartolo Colon, or Randy Johnson?

10. What pitcher has the most career victories without a 20-win season: Dennis Martinez, Frank Tanana, Kenny Rogers, or Charlie Hough?

CROSSWORD PUZZLE 3

Answer on page 73

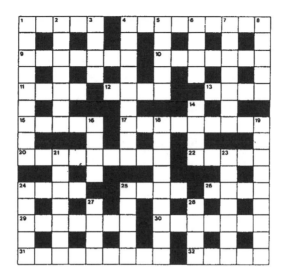

ACROSS

1 Do what Rickey Henderson did so well

4 Pitcher Dennis Martinez hailed from this country

9 They make the calls on the field

10 A grand slam may earn a player a standing _____

11 A baseball player's weak spot, Achilles' _____

12 Former Expo _____ Calderon

13 Tommie _____ is remembered for a couple of spectacular catches for the Mets in the 1969 World Series

15 Hall of Famer known as "Cap"

17 Beats a throw to first base (3wds.)

20 Todd Helton of Rockies wears this uniform number

22 Many youngsters have a _____ of playing in the majors

24 Caps

25 Distance a base runner takes from first base

26 Remain in contention, _____ alive

29 1997 World Series champs

30 Only non-U.S. team that's captured a world championship (two, in fact)

31 An outfielder, he played for the Dodgers' World Series teams in 1959, 1963, 1965, and 1966

32 Pitcher Bruce _____ was with the Pirates when they won the World Series in 1971 and 1979

DOWN

1 Lefties
2 Nolan Ryan was dubbed "The _____"
3 Barry _____in was a great shortstop for the Reds
4 Home of the minor league Sounds in the Pacific Coast League
5 Yaz was the majors' last Triple _____ winner
6 Away from home, on the _____
7 _____ __ the mouth arouses suspicion of the spitball (2wds.)

8 A free pass is nicknamed as _____ Oakley
14 Charlie Sheen played "_____ Thing" in Major League
16 Right field is indicated by this number by scorers
18 Former Angels owner who sang in the movies
19 Onetime pitcher for whom a form of arm surgery is named
21 Experienced ball player
23 Widens
24 Dinger
25 What the letter L indicates
27 Jose _____ won 21 games for Houston in 1999
28 Pitcher _____ Bedard was a 15-game winner with the Orioles in 2006

Team Identification

Answers on page 74

Identify the team each of the listed major leaguers played their first game for.

Player	Team	Player	Team
Ryne Sandberg	_____	Curt Schilling	_____
Joe Torre	_____	Juan Pierre	_____
Derrek Lee	_____	Trevor Hoffman	_____
Roberto Alomar	_____	Johnny Damon	_____
Jeff Kent	_____	Joe Carter	_____
Gaylord Perry	_____	Orlando Cabrera	_____
Sammy Sosa	_____	Scott Rolen	_____
Willie Randolph	_____	Bobby Bonilla	_____
Reggie Jackson	_____	Gary Sheffield	_____

QUIZ 7

Answers on page 74

True or False

Collect four points for each true or false question you answer correctly.

1. Reggie Jackson is the only player in World Series history to hit three home runs in one game.

2. Jim Palmer won 268 games during his 19-year major league career but never tossed a no-hitter.

3. Albert Pujols has never struck out 100 or more times in a season.

4. Eric Gagne is the only reliever to save 50 or more games in a season without blowing a save opportunity.

5. Hank Aaron holds the National League record for most years leading the league in home runs with eight.

6. When elected to the Hall of Fame in 1972, Sandy Koufax received less than 90 percent of the voting tally.

7. Ted Williams is the only player in baseball history to win two Triple Crowns.

8. Despite scoring 1,882 career runs, Hall of Famer Tris Speaker never led the league in runs scored.

9. Pete Rose totaled 1,566 walks during his career without ever drawing 100 or more in a single season.

10. Jim Bunning was the second pitcher in the major league history to record 3,000 or more strikeouts.

11. Babe Ruth and Lou Gehrig are the only teammates to drive in 150 or more runs in the same season.

12. Prince Fielder was the youngest player in major league history to club 50 or more home runs in a season.

13. Randy Johnson is the only pitcher to record 2,000 or more strikeouts for two different teams.

14. In 1982, when Rickey Henderson set a single-season mark with 130 stolen bases, he also set the record for most times being caught attempting to steal.

15. Tony La Russa is the only manager to win 1,000 or more games in both the American and National leagues.

16. Hall of Fame catcher Carlton Fisk holds the record for most games caught in a career.

17. Randy Hundley is the only catcher in baseball history to catch 160 games in a single-season.

18. Among 300-game winners since 1900, Don Sutton is the only pitcher with 300 or more lifetime victories without ever leading his league in wins during his career.

19. Joe Torre is the only manager with 2,000 or more career victories who captured a league MVP Award as a player.

20. Bobby Bonds is the only player in major league history to strikeout 180 or more times in a season and maintain a batting average of .300 or better.

21. Ted Williams won three American League MVP Awards during his career.

22. Joe Carter hit his World Series–winning home run in 1993 off Phillies' pitcher Mitch Williams.

23. When Roger Maris clubbed 61 home runs for the Yankees in 1961, it was the only time during his career that he hit 30 or more in a season.

24. Ichiro Suzuki is the only player to hit an inside-the-park home run in the All-Star Game.

25. Despite 310 career saves in the major leagues, Rich Gossage never registered 30 or more saves in a season.

THEY SAID IT . . .

"When I was a small boy in Kansas, a friend of mine and I went fishing.... I told him I wanted to be a real Major League Baseball Player, a genuine professional like Honus Wagner. My friend said that he'd like to be President of the United States. Neither of us got our wish."
—Former President Dwight D. Eisenhower

"I'm never satisfied. I can't stand satisfaction. To me, greatness comes from that quest for perfection."
—Hall of Famer Mike Schmidt

"You spend a good piece of your life gripping a baseball and in the end it turns out that it was the other way around all the time." *—Former pitcher Jim Bouton*

1. Jacoby Ellsbury leads off the contest for the Red Sox facing Yankees' pitcher CC Sabathia. The left-hander throws two wild pitches to start the game. Joe Girardi, the disgruntled Yankees manager, goes to the mound to change pitchers. The umpires properly disallow Girardi to do this since

Answers on page 77

Sabathia must pitch to the first batter or his substitute until such batter is put out or reaches base. True or False?

2. The Rangers have the bases loaded in the bottom of the ninth with the score tied 5-5 and one out when Ian Kinsler hits a shot over the center-field wall. The runners from third and second cross the plate. Kinsler, however, passes Josh Hamilton, the runner on first, and is called out. The umpires correctly end the game with the Rangers winning, 6-5. True or False?

3. The Tigers have runners on first and third. The Royals infield is playing shallow to make a play at the plate. Tigers' batter Miguel Cabrera smashes a hard grounder between the legs of first baseman Billy Butler, who deflects the ball into the path of Ryan Raburn, the runner going from first to second. Raburn intentionally kicks the ball as it nears him. Because Butler deflected the ball, Raburn should not be called out and the ball should remain alive and in play. True or False?

4. Concerning question No. 3, the umpires should call both Raburn and Cabrera out. True or False?

5. The Cardinals are hosting the Padres in St. Louis. The Cards have Skip Schumaker on first when Albert Pujols hits a Clayton Richard pitch that bounces into the stands for a double down the right field line. Schumaker, going with the pitch, misses second base and is between second and third when the ball goes over the wall. At that point he advances to and touches third base. Realizing he missed second base, he attempts to return to second to retouch but the third base umpire does not allow him to do so since Schumaker touched a base beyond the missed base after the ball became dead. The umpire did the right thing. True or False?

6. Gordon Beckham is on first base for the White Sox when Carlos Quentin hits a ground ball to Angels' shortstop Erick Aybar who tosses to Howie Kendrick at second retiring Beckham. But for some reason Beckham continues to third. Kendrick throws to third and the ball goes into dead-ball territory. At the time of Kendrick's throw, Quentin was on first base and is sent to third. The Angels argue that Beckham, who was retired, confused the defense by running to third; and because of that, Quentin should also be called out. The umpires should support the Angels in this argument and call Quentin out. True or False?

7. With runners on first and second, David Ortiz of the Red Sox rips a vicious liner off the center field wall at Fenway Park. Both runners score easily, but a stitch in the ball breaks and the ball comes partially apart. The Blue Jays argue that because the ball came apart, the ball should be dead and the runners should not score. The umps correctly agree as they return the runners to load the bases. True or False?

8. With the bases empty, Mets' pitcher Johan Santana decides to pitch from the stretch. He comes to a stop during his first four pitches to Phillies' first baseman Ryan Howard, who works the count to 2-2. On the next offering, Santana does not come to a stop in the set position and whiffs the surprised Phillies' batter. Philadelphia manager Charlie Manuel argues that Santana must come to a complete stop in the set position. The umpires say that is necessary only with runners on base. The umpires are correct. True or False?

9. Jack Cust of the A's swings and chops a high bounding ball down the first base line. The Twins' first baseman, Justin Morneau, comes in to field the ball several feet in front of the bag. Both his feet are in fair territory as he reaches across the line in foul territory to field the ball. This is a fair ball because Morneau's feet were in fair territory. True or False?

10. Hunter Pence is standing in the batter's box for the Astros when a Chad Billingsley pitch grazes the sleeve of Pence's undershirt but not his arm. The plate umpire sends Pence to first because the pitch hit him. Dodgers' manager Joe Torre argues that since Pence was not actually hit by the pitch, he should not be awarded first base. The umps should support Torre's argument. True or False?

Fill in the Blank

Answers on page 78

A. Besides No. 42, which is retired by all major league clubs in honor of Jackie Robinson, the Yankees have 16 uniform numbers retired (through 2009). See how many players you can identify with their number.

Note: Two players had No. 8

_____ No. 1		_____ No. 10	
_____ No. 3		_____ No. 15	
_____ No. 4		_____ No. 16	
_____ No. 5		_____ No. 23	
_____ No. 7		_____ No. 32	
_____ No. 8		_____ No. 37	
_____ No. 8		_____ No. 44	
_____ No. 9		_____ No. 49	

B. Identify the eight major league players with 3,000 hits and 400 home runs.

_____ 755 home runs, 3,771 hits
_____ 660 home runs, 3,283 hits
_____ 569 home runs, 3,020 hits
_____ 504 home runs, 3,255 hits
_____ 475 home runs, 3,630 hits
_____ 465 home runs, 3,110 hits
_____ 452 home runs, 3,419 hits
_____ 431 home runs, 3,184 hits

PHOTO QUIZ 2

Answers on page 79

Collect five points for each player you identify correctly.

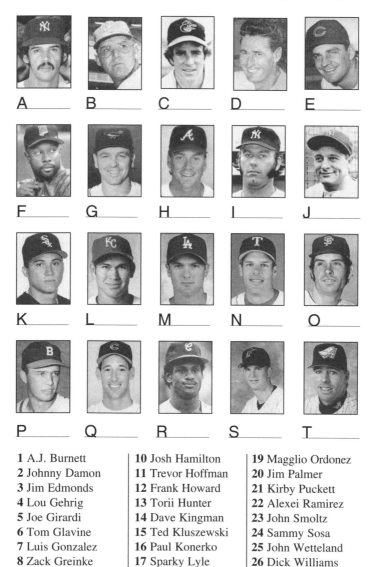

A ___ B ___ C ___ D ___ E ___

F ___ G ___ H ___ I ___ J ___

K ___ L ___ M ___ N ___ O ___

P ___ Q ___ R ___ S ___ T ___

1 A.J. Burnett
2 Johnny Damon
3 Jim Edmonds
4 Lou Gehrig
5 Joe Girardi
6 Tom Glavine
7 Luis Gonzalez
8 Zack Greinke
9 Ron Guidry

10 Josh Hamilton
11 Trevor Hoffman
12 Frank Howard
13 Torii Hunter
14 Dave Kingman
15 Ted Kluszewski
16 Paul Konerko
17 Sparky Lyle
18 Eddie Mathews

19 Magglio Ordonez
20 Jim Palmer
21 Kirby Puckett
22 Alexei Ramirez
23 John Smoltz
24 Sammy Sosa
25 John Wetteland
26 Dick Williams
27 Ted Williams

QUIZ 8

Answers on page 79

MVP Award Winners

1. Ten players have won three or more league MVP Awards since the Baseball Writers Association of America began voting for winners in 1931. Collect one point for each three-time MVP you can identify.

2. From 1931 through 2009 there have been 15 unanimous MVP selections. Collect ten points if you identify five of those 15 players.

3. Which one of the following players never won an MVP Award: Roberto Clemente, Harmon Killebrew, Barry Larkin, or Eddie Murray?

4. Since 1931, Carl Hubbell was the first pitcher to win multiple MVP Awards. Who is the only other pitcher to accomplish this feat: Sandy Koufax, Hal Newhouser, Bob Gibson, or Roger Clemens?

5. Nine different players from the Boston Red Sox have won an American League MVP Award. Collect ten points if you can identify five of these players.

6. Who was the first player to win consecutive MVP Awards: Lou Gehrig, Joe DiMaggio, Jimmie Foxx, Roy Campanella, or Stan Musial?

7. Excluding pitchers, nine switch-hitters have captured league MVP honors. Collect ten points if you can identify five of these players. A clue: eight of the nine are National Leaguers.

8. Who was the first relief pitcher to win a league MVP Award: Willie Hernandez, Jim Konstanty, Rollie Fingers, or Dennis Eckersley?

9. Only two players have won Rookie of the Year and the MVP Award in the same season. Collect five points for each of these players you can identify.

10. Before Joe Mauer captured the 2009 American League Most Valuable Player Award, who was the last catcher to win an MVP: Ivan Rodriguez, Johnny Bench, Thurman Munson, or Mike Piazza?

QUIZ 9

Answers on page 81

Who Am I?

1. I won two All-Star game MVP Awards, two League Championship Series MVP Awards, and one league MVP honor. I collected 200 hits in a season six times. I came up as a third baseman before becoming a regular first baseman and winning four Gold Glove Awards. From late 1975 and midway through the 1983 season, I played 1,207 consecutive games. Who am I?

2. Through 2009, I am the only catcher to collect 200 hits in one season. I won Rookie of the Year honors after hitting .318 with 35 home runs in my first full season. I clubbed 30 or more homers in a season nine times and 40 twice. I finished my career with a .308 batting average and 427 homers, including a record 396 by a catcher. Who am I?

3. I was a 20-game winner in both the American and National leagues during my career. I never won a Cy Young Award but was voted MVP in an LCS and a World Series. I struck out 300 or more batters in a season three times and more than 3,000 for my career. Who am I?

4. I have the highest fielding percentage among shortstops with 1,000 or more games played. I won 11 Gold Glove Awards and six fielding titles. I have more than 350 stolen bases and 2,700 career hits with a .273 batting average. Who am I?

5. I am a former league home run king and three-time batting champion. I won seven Gold Glove Awards in the outfield and was a five-time All-Star. I played 17 years in the majors and finished with a .313 batting average, 471 doubles, and 383 home runs. I grew up in Maple Ridge, British Columbia. Who am I?

6. I clubbed 493 career home runs during my 19 years in the majors and captured two home run titles—one in each league. I hit 30 or more homers in a season with five different teams and 200-plus in the A.L. and N.L. I played on one World Series winner. Who am I?

7. I broke into the major leagues at age 21 in 1993. I won one home run title, led the league in RBI once, and am a former batting champion—but I never won a Triple Crown. I drove in 100 or more runs in 12 of my first 17 seasons and have more than 500 doubles and home runs, including more than 20 grand slams, in my career. Who am I?

8. I began my career as a catcher before becoming a Gold Glove–winning infielder. I finished my career with more than 3,000 hits and am one of only 14 major leaguers with more than 600 career doubles. I stole 414 bases, including a league-leading total in 1994, and played my entire 20-year career with one club. Who am I?

9. I pitched 22 years in the big leagues, winning 287 games. I rank ninth all time in shutouts with 60 and fifth in strikeouts with 3,701. I completed 242 games while helping my teams to two World Series titles. I pitched a no-hitter in 1977 for the Texas Rangers. Who am I?

10. I played 14 seasons in the American League, winning one home run title and clubbing 271 homers—which I referred to as "taters"—during my career. I called my glove "Black Beauty" and captured eight Gold Glove Awards for my fielding excellence at first base. My nickname was "Boomer" for my booming home runs, and I wore a necklace that I said was composed of "second basemen's teeth." Who am I?

DID YOU KNOW . . .

• . . . that there are three players with the first name "Reggie" who hit 300 or more career home runs in the major leagues? Reggie Jackson hit 563, Reggie Smith clubbed 314, and Reggie Sanders, 305.

• . . . that there have been four managers to win the Manager of the Year Award in both leagues? They include Lou Piniella (Mariners/Cubs), Tony LaRussa (White Sox/A's/Cardinals), Bobby Cox (Blue Jays/Braves), and Jim Leyland (Pirates/Tigers).

• . . . that Babe Herman is the only player to hit for the cycle twice in one season? He did it on May 18 and July 24, 1931, for the Dodgers.

BASEBALL BY THE RULES

4

Answers on page 81

1. With a count of one ball and two strikes, Chris Carpenter throws a sharp breaking pitch that fools Brewers' batter Ryan Braun who starts to swing, then tries to hold back. Home-plate umpire Chuck Meriwether rules strike three on the swing, but Braun disagrees. He asks Meriwether to get help by asking the first base umpire. Should Meriwether ask his partner?

2. Nick Markakis of the Orioles hits a grand slam with two outs. But on appeal, Markakis is called out for missing first base. How many runs score?

3. With runners on first and second and no outs, the Reds' Jay Bruce hits a pop fly in the area of third base. Plate umpire Tim Welke yells, "Infield Fly if fair." The ball falls untouched in front of third base in fair territory, then rolls foul. Should Bruce be ruled out?

4. Cleveland's Shin-Soo Choo lashes a shot into the left center field gap at Yankee Stadium. As he rounds third attempting an inside-the-park home run, he trips over the bag and turns his ankle. The third base coach helps Choo to his feet as he retreats gingerly to third. Choo is removed from the game. The Indians want to use designated hitter Travis Hafner as a pinch-runner. If you were the ump, how would you handle this?

5. With one out and Toronto runners on first and third, Vernon Wells is batting with a 3-2 count. He swings and misses, and the pitch eludes White Sox's catcher A. J. Pierzynski's catcher's mitt, hits him in the mask, and deflects behind his chest protector where it becomes lodged. Pierzynski has no idea where the ball is, and as he darts around looking for it the Blue Jays' runner from third scores, the runner from first advances to third, and Wells, the batter, goes to second. How would you straighten out this mess?

6. With two strikes on him, the Phils' Shane Victorino decides to surprise the Astros' defense and squares around to bunt. Astros' pitcher Wandy Rodriguez uncorks a wild pitch high and inside. Victorino tries desperately to avoid the pitch, but the ball hits his bat and rolls foul. Should Victorino be called out for bunting foul?

7. The Mariners' Felix Hernandez has a no-hitter in the ninth with one out. With Dustin Pedroia on second, J. D. Drew hits a ground ball between second and third that strikes Pedroia. Umpire Dale Scott calls Pedroia out for interference. Is Hernandez's no-hitter still intact?

8. Mets' pitcher John Maine has a problem releasing the ball and fires it into the ground. The ball bounces once and enters the strike zone. Cubs' batter Alfonso Soriano sends the bouncer into left field for a base hit. If you were the ump, should you allow the hit?

9. Evan Longoria hits a ground ball to Yankee first baseman Mark Teixeira. Pitcher A. J. Burnett comes over to take the toss from Teixeira, but before he receives the ball, he collides with Longoria as they both converge on the first-base bag. First base umpire Bruce Dreckman calls obstruction on Burnett since Teixeira had not yet released the ball. Did the umpire make the proper call?

10. With the Marlins' Hanley Ramirez on second, Chris Coghlan hits a ground ball to Colorado shortstop Troy Tulowitzki, who throws to first to retire Coghlan. Ramirez rounds third and races for home. First baseman Todd Helton's throw home hits Coghlan, who is not in the batter-runner's three-foot lane. Should Ramirez be declared out at the plate?

You Make the Call . . .   *Answer on page 82*

On August 8, 2001, during an A's/Red Sox game in Oakland, Johnny Damon of the A's hit a fair ball down the right-field line that rolled—and lodged solidly—into an empty cup lying on the field. If you were the umpire, how would you make the call?

PLAYER IDENTIFICATION

Answers on page 82

How many players can you name correctly with only one clue given for their identity?

1. I am the only major league pitcher to throw a no-hitter on opening day. _____

2. I am the only player with 3,000 or more career hits and fewer than 50 home runs. _____

3. I was the 3,000th strikeout victim for both Bob Gibson and Nolan Ryan. _____

4. I collected the most base hits (1,274) at old Yankee Stadium. _____

5. Among players eligible for election to the Hall of Fame, I am the only player to win four batting titles and not be elected to the Hall of Fame. _____

6. I hold the record for most career doubles with 792 during my 22 seasons in the majors. _____

7. I am the only player to hit a home run for his 3,000th career hit. _____

8. I am the only player in big league history to steal 100 or more bases in three consecutive seasons. _____

9. I was a 20-game winner eight times in nine seasons during the 1970s. _____

10. Besides Ty Cobb, I am the only player to hit .400 in back-to-back seasons since 1900. _____

11. I am the only pitcher with two 20-strikeout games in the major leagues. _____

12. I am the only manager with 2,000 or more career wins who has a .600 winning percentage. _____

13. I am the only player to win a batting title during the 1970s, 1980s, and 1990s. _____

14. I am the only pitcher in baseball history with 100 or more career shutouts. _____

15. During the 1990s I collected the most hits (1,754) and doubles (364). _____

CROSSWORD PUZZLE 4

Answer on page 83

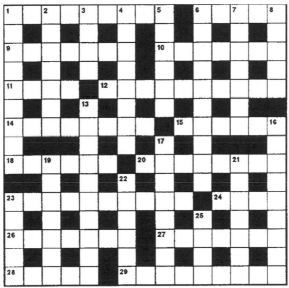

ACROSS

1 He skippered the A.L. champion Rays

6 Carlos _____ was 191-191 as manager of the Blue Jays

9 The Phillie Phanatic and San Diego Chicken

10 Charley _____ is now the main radio voice of the Dodgers

11 Vulnerable area for a ballplayer, Achilles _____

12 Zack Greinke was A.L.'s Cy _____ _____ winner in '09 (2wds.)

14 Bob Feller was _____ (famous) for his fastball

15 An RBI hitter likes to have runners _____ (on base) when he comes to the plate

18 When a team scores many runs in one inning, its offense _____ (explodes)

20 _____ _____ (2wds.) former union boss Marvin Miller, baseball salaries eventually soared

23 Rockies player who led majors with a .372 batting average in 2000

24 Don Kessinger and Glenn Beckert once formed the keystone combination for this club

26 A pitch that splits the middle of the strike zone is said to be down ___ ____ (2wds.)

27 Hudson played second base for the Dodgers in 2009

28 Sometimes a pitcher ____ up (doesn't throw as hard) against certain batters if his team has a big lead

29 Harry Agganis was dubbed " ___ ____ Greek" (2wds.)

DOWN

1 Legendary Native American who had his Olympic medals taken away because he played in the majors

2 Theo ____ calls the shots in Boston

3 Former Royals speedster ____ Otis

4 In the old days, "bird dogs" were used to _____ new talent

5 Defeating narrowly, ____ out

6 One of Babe Ruth's nicknames

7 Johan ____ of the Mets

8 Televised a game

13 Bats from both sides of the plate

16 Pitches sidearm (2wds.)

17 Full first name of the "Splendid Splinter"

19 Players ____ (remove their uniforms) in the clubhouse after a game

21 Johnny Vander Meer ___ (shocked) the baseball world with two straight no-hitters in 1938

22 2008–2009 N.L. MVP ____ Pujols

23 Ernie Banks earned the ____ (nickname) of "Mr. Cub"

25 A team that finishes back in the standings is an ___-ran

Name That Hall of Famer
Answers on page 84

A. I had a losing record in my 12 seasons in the majors. I won one Cy Young Award and was a six-time All-Star who led the league in saves five times with a lifetime total of 300. Who am I?

B. I am the only player with 3,000 career hits and three batting titles with a lifetime batting average below .300. Who am I?

QUIZ 10

Answers on page 84

Rookie Achievements

1. Besides Ichiro Suzuki, who is the only other rookie to win a league batting title: Fred Lynn, Rod Carew, Tony Oliva, or Ted Williams?

2. Who holds the record for most stolen bases by a rookie: Tim Raines, Vince Coleman, Eric Davis, or Rickey Henderson?

3. Frank Robinson and Wally Berger hold the N.L. record for most homers by a rookie: 38. Mark McGwire holds the A.L. mark with 49. Whose record did McGwire break: Al Rosen, Rudy York, Lou Gehrig, or Jose Canseco?

4. What rookie holds the record for the longest consecutive-game hitting streak: Sandy Alomar, Albert Pujols, Jerome Walton, or Benito Santiago?

5. Who holds the record for most saves by a rookie pitcher with 37: Jonathan Papelbon, John Wetteland, Todd Worrell, or Kazuhiro Sasaki?

6. The A.L. record for most RBI by a rookie is 145 set by Ted Williams of the Red Sox in 1939. Who holds the N.L. mark for most RBI with 130: Mike Piazza, Albert Pujols, Prince Fielder, or Johnny Bench?

7. In 1984, Seattle Mariners first baseman Alvin Davis won the A.L. Rookie of the Year Award. What teammate finished second to Davis in the voting that year: Ken Griffey, Jr., Edgar Martinez, Mark Langston, or Harold Reynolds?

8. Fourteen players collected 200 or more hits during their rookie season. Collect ten points if you can identify five of these players.

9. Who was the last rookie pitcher, through 2009, to throw a no-hitter: Jon Lester, Jonathan Sanchez, Clay Buchholz, or Anibal Sanchez?

10. In 1959, Larry Sherry became the first rookie to win a World Series MVP Award. What other player later accomplished this feat: Livan Hernandez, Troy Glaus, Jose Rijo, or Derek Jeter?

Fill in the Blank

Answers on page 86

• *Four players have won a league Rookie of the Year Award with one team and an MVP Award with another club. Identify the clubs the following players won their awards with.*

Player	Rookie Team	MVP Team(s)
Frank Robinson	_____	_____
		_____
Orlando Cepeda	_____	_____
Dick Allen	_____	_____
Andre Dawson	_____	_____

• *Through 2009 and excluding pitchers who won the Cy Young and MVP Award in the same season, there have been 18 occurrences when the Cy Young winner and MVP recipient came from the same team. How many of these players can you identify?*

Year	Team	MVP	Cy Young
1957	Milwaukee Braves	_____	_____
1959	Chicago White Sox	_____	_____
1960	Pittsburgh Pirates	_____	_____
1961	New York Yankees	_____	_____
1962	L.A. Dodgers	_____	_____
1967	Boston Red Sox	_____	_____
1974	L.A. Dodgers	_____	_____
1980	Philadelphia Phillies	_____	_____
1982	Milwaukee Brewers	_____	_____
1984	Chicago Cubs	_____	_____
1988	L.A. Dodgers	_____	_____
1990	Oakland A's	_____	_____
1990	Pittsburgh Pirates	_____	_____
1991	Atlanta Braves	_____	_____
1993	Chicago White Sox	_____	_____
2002	Oakland A's	_____	_____
2005	St. Louis Cardinals	_____	_____
2006	Minnesota Twins	_____	_____

CROSSWORD PUZZLE 5

Answer on page 87

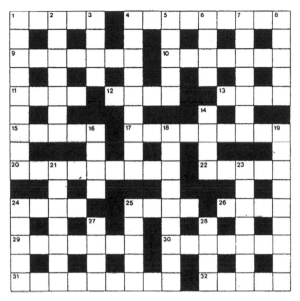

ACROSS

1 Switch-hitting catcher Varitek

4 Pitcher Chris Carpenter is this club's ace

9 Glasses and contact lenses are kinds of ____

10 Baseball's onetime "Spaceman" who pitched for Boston Red Sox and Montreal Expos

11 On the road, ____ from home

12 Braun, left fielder with the Brewers, won N.L. Rookie of the Year honors in 2007

13 Randy Johnson is known as "The Big ___"

15 Slang for a home run

17 A bench coach is primarily an _____ to the manager

20 Home of the minor league Red Wings

22 Defeated narrowly: ____ out

24 The thickest part of the bat

25 Touches a base runner for an out

26 Felipe ____ was manager in Montreal and San Francisco

29 An infielder with the Dodgers, "Junior" was the

National League's top rookie in 1953
30 A team may suffer a ____ after a tough loss
31 Home city where four future Hall of Famers (Early Wynn, Bob Lemon, Bob Feller, and Hal Newhouser) were once together on the same pitching staff
32 Former baseball commissioner Ueberroth

DOWN
1 He homered to give the Jays their second world championship over the Phillies in 1993
2 Actor Jimmy ____ played a pitcher in the movie *The Monte Stratton Story*
3 All teams ____ strong pitching if they expect to win
4 Outfielder with the Brewers who was an All-Star in 2008

5 Hall of Famer Yount who won A.L. MVP Award in 1982 and 1989
6 Not playing
7 Where Bobby Cox calls the shots
8 "____" Lou Piniella
14 A cable sports network
16 Pitcher Rick ____ was an All-Star in 1998 and 2001
18 Was in a slump
19 Atlanta's ballpark is named after him
21 A curveball is called "Uncle ____"
23 Game for which no tickets remain
24 A team with a ____ number is close to clinching
25 Home of the 2008 A.L. pennant-winning Rays
27 Number worn by "Joltin' Joe"
28 A ____ sign tells a base runner to hold

Name the Players

Answers on page 87

A major league player has not won the Triple Crown (leading the league in homers, RBI, and batting average) since 1967 when Boston's Carl Yastrzemski did it. Through 2009, two active players have won league titles in homers, RBI, and batting average without winning the Triple Crown. Who are these two sluggers?

1. The Giants are batting in the top of the fifth inning. With Pablo Sandoval on first base and one out, Fred Lewis homers off Clayton Kershaw of the Dodgers. As the runners are circling the bases, Lewis passes Sandoval between second and third base. Sandoval should be called out and Lewis should be allowed to complete his home run trot since he hit the ball out of the park. True or False?

Answers on page 87

2. With one out, the Red Sox have David Ortiz on third base and Mike Lowell on first when Jason Varitek hits a high pop foul near the stands along the first base line. Justin Morneau, the Twins' first baseman, leaps over the railing, catches the ball in the air, then falls into the stands. The umpire should call the play "dead" and allow each runner one base, which would score Ortiz. True or False?

3. The Mets are batting in a game against the Pirates. With a 2-2 count on David Wright, Jeff Francoeur, the runner on third, is caught in a rundown between third and home. In the ensuing action, Francoeur is obstructed by Pirates' third baseman Andy LaRoche as Francoeur attempts to return to third. Even though Francoeur was obstructed while returning to third base, he should be awarded home by the umpires. True or False?

4. With Chris Getz on first base, David DeJesus is batting for the Royals with one out and a count of two balls and two strikes. DeJesus swings and misses a Kerry Wood fastball while Getz attempts to steal second base. The momentum of DeJesus' swing carries him into Cleveland catcher Lou Marson, who is unable to complete his throw to second. Because of DeJesus' interference, Getz should also be called out. True or False?

5. In the top of the seventh inning at Wrigley Field in Chicago, Prince Fielder of the Brewers hits a three-run homer to put Milwaukee ahead 5-3. With one out in the bottom of the seventh, a heavy downpour forces the umpires to call the game. The Cubs luck out because the score now reverts back to the last completed inning, giving the Cubs a 3-2 win. True or False?

6. The Angels and Rangers are hooked up in a real sizzler at Angel Stadium when members of the Angels' bench continue to argue loudly about umpire C.B. Bucknor's strike zone. Bucknor informs Angels' manager Mike Scioscia that he must clear his bench of all nonstarters. Scioscia has the right to bring back any player he wishes to use as a substitute. True or False?

7. Mark Reynolds of the Diamondbacks hits a long drive to right field that bounces out of Rockies right fielder Brad Hawpe's glove and into the stands in fair territory. Reynolds should be awarded two bases. True or False?

8. As Tampa Bay's Ben Zobrist swings and misses a Felix Hernandez pitch, the ball strikes him on the arm. This is a dead ball, and Zobrist should be given first base. True or False?

9. The Reds have Joey Votto on first base when Ramon Hernandez hits a rope that strikes Votto on the bag. First-base umpire Wally Bell rules the play dead and calls Votto out. True or False?

10. Alex Rios of the White Sox drives a ball into the right-center field gap at Yankee Stadium in New York. Yankee center fielder Brett Gardner throws his glove at the ball. Gardner's glove fails to hit the ball, but because he threw his glove at it, Rios should be awarded third base. True or False?

You Make the Call . . .   *Answers on page 89*

With two out and two strikes, Ichiro Suzuki swings and misses at a pitch in the dirt. The pitch bounces off the catcher Jorge Posada into the air, and Ichiro's bat strikes the ball, causing it to roll into foul territory. What is the call?

QUIZ 11

Answers on page 89

Streaks

1. Since 1900 and through 2009, four players have put together hitting streaks of 40 or more games in the major leagues. Collect 10 points if you can identify three of them.

2. Cal Ripken holds the major league and A.L. mark for most consecutive games played with 2,632, but who holds the National League record at 1,207: Billy Williams, Stan Musial, Pete Rose, or Steve Garvey?

3. Who is the only active player to maintain a streak of more than 1,000 consecutive games played during his career: Paul Konerko, Miguel Tejada, Ichiro Suzuki, or Albert Pujols?

4. What player holds the record for most consecutive games with an RBI at 17: Manny Ramirez, Mike Piazza, Ray Grimes, or Hack Wilson?

5. The big league record for reaching base the most consecutive games via hit, walk, or hit-by-pitch is 84, held by what player: Joe DiMaggio, Ted Williams, Barry Bonds, or Babe Ruth?

6. What batter holds the record for most consecutive games with a base on balls with 22: Mark McGwire, Gene Tenace, Roy Cullenbine, or Sammy Sosa?

7. What pitcher holds the record for most consecutive perfect innings pitched: Harvey Haddix, Mark Buehrle, Sandy Koufax, or David Cone?

8. Who is the only pitcher to toss six consecutive shutouts: Bob Gibson, Orel Hershiser, Walter Johnson, Don Drysdale, or Luis Tiant?

9. The major league record for most consecutive games with 10 or more strikeouts by a pitcher is eight. What strikeout specialist holds this mark: Pedro Martinez, Nolan Ryan, Randy Johnson, or Dwight Gooden?

10. Through the 2009 season, three players had hit a home run in eight successive games in the majors. Collect 10 points if you can identify two of these three sluggers. A clue: Two players did it in the A.L. and one in the N.L.

Name the Manager

Answers on page 90

A. There were 20 World Series sweeps through 2009. How many managers can you name who led their club to a Series whitewash?

Winning Year	Losing Team	Winning Team	Manager
1907	Cubs	Tigers	_____
1914	Bos. Braves	Phil. A's	_____
1922	N.Y. Giants	Yankees	_____
1927	Yankees	Pirates	_____
1928	Yankees	Cardinals	_____
1932	Yankees	Cubs	_____
1938	Yankees	Cubs	_____
1939	Yankees	Reds	_____
1950	Yankees	Phillies	_____
1954	N.Y. Giants	Indians	_____
1963	L.A. Dodgers	Yankees	_____
1966	Orioles	L.A. Dodgers	_____
1976	Reds	Yankees	_____
1989	Oak. A's	S.F. Giants	_____
1990	Reds	Oak. A's	_____
1998	Yankees	Padres	_____
1999	Yankees	Atl. Braves	_____
2004	Red Sox	Cardinals	_____
2005	White Sox	Astros	_____
2007	Red Sox	Rockies	_____

B. Billy Martin finished his career with a 1,253-1,013 won-lost record as a manager for five different big league clubs. How many teams can you identify that Martin managed?

C. I played 14 seasons in the majors as an outfielder, playing on seven World Series–winning Yankee teams. I managed eight years in the majors, including the 1966 World Series champion Baltimore Orioles. Who am I?

PHOTO QUIZ 3

Answers on page 91

Collect five points for each player you identify correctly.

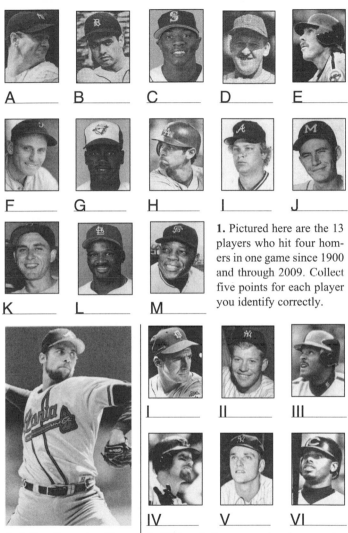

A _____ B _____ C _____ D _____ E _____

F _____ G _____ H _____ I _____ J _____

K _____ L _____ M _____

1. Pictured here are the 13 players who hit four homers in one game since 1900 and through 2009. Collect five points for each player you identify correctly.

I _____ II _____ III _____

IV _____ V _____ VI _____

2. Collect five points if you can identify this former Cy Young Award winner.

3. Pictured above are six players who had a 50-homer season in the major leagues. Collect five points for each of these sluggers you can identify.

QUIZ 12

Answers on page 91

World Series

1. Besides former Dodger Chuck Essegian, who is the only other player to club two home runs as a pinch-hitter in one World Series: Kirk Gibson, Bernie Carbo, Hideki Matsui, or Pat Burrell?

2. From 1955 through 2009 there have been 12 different New York Yankees who have captured World Series MVP honors. Collect 10 points if you can identify seven of these 12 players.

3. Who is the only player to get 10 or more hits in one World Series twice in his career, but with different teams: Pete Rose, Dave Justice, Paul Molitor, or Steve Garvey?

4. Don Larsen (1956), David Wells (1998), and David Cone (1999) are three Yankee pitchers who threw a perfect game and won a World Series contest in the same season. Who is the only other pitcher to accomplish this feat: Randy Johnson, Sandy Koufax, Tom Browning, or Jim Hunter?

5. Who is the only player to hit a World Series home run with three different teams: Manny Ramirez, Eddie Murray, Matt Williams, or Jim Eisenreich?

6. Through 2009 there have been 14 walk-off home runs in World Series history. Name six of the 14 players to hit game-ending homers in the Fall Classic and collect ten points.

7. Who is the only pitcher to have two complete-game victories in a Game 7 World Series: Sandy Koufax, Jack Morris, Ralph Terry, or Bob Gibson?

8. What player holds the record for collecting 10 hits in a four-game World Series sweep: Chris Sabo, Babe Ruth, Jermaine Dye, or Derek Jeter?

9. Who is the only relief pitcher to strike out 10 or more batters in a World Series game: Rollie Fingers, Livan Hernandez, Moe Drabowski, or Bruce Kison?

10. Besides Chase Utley, who is the only other player to hit three home runs in one World Series against the same pitcher: Mickey Mantle, Willie Aikens, Yogi Berra, or Johnny Bench?

CROSSWORD PUZZLE 6

Answer on page 92

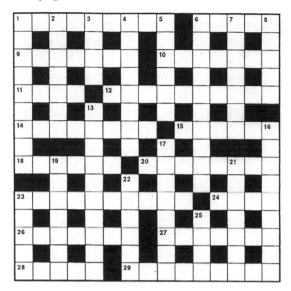

ACROSS

1 Roger Kahn's book about the old Brooklyn Dodgers (with 18 Across) (3wds.)
6 Tony _____ was once a manager in Kansas City
9 He's Cards' skipper
10 Wins or loses a series of games in succession
11 The Braves' _____per Jones
12 Former Gold Glove center fielder for Angels and Cardinals
14 Encircle
15 Shutouts
18 See 1 Across
20 Major league clubs are idle this month
23 Homered: _____ _____ fences (2wds.)
24 Aaron or Bauer
26 Pitcher Don _____ starred for the Reds in the 1970s
27 A player may experience this after being beaned
28 Pitch
29 Men at first and third, ___ __ _____ the corners (2wds.)

DOWN

1 Baseball games on television
2 In _____ (previous) times, pitchers were allowed to throw the spitball
3 Eject a player from a game

4 Positions where players are situated on the field
5 George _____ was National League MVP in 1977 with Cincinnati
6 He was a 21-game winner for the A's in 2001
7 Former Blue Jays and Twins outfielder Stewart, who stole 51 bases for Toronto in 1998
8 Takes chances
13 Ex-Reds second baseman who won consecutive Gold Gloves in 1999–2000

16 Fan (2wds.)
17 The Toronto Blue Jays once had a farm club in this Connecticut city
19 Former Red Sox third baseman who won an A.L. batting title in 2003, Bill _____
21 Slang for batting helmets
22 One who oversees a baseball publication
23 Batting _____ are enclosed frameworks used in practice before games
25 Base on balls: _____ pass

Team Identification
Answers on page 93

A. Through 2009 there were five players who had put together a 200-hit season in both leagues. Identify the clubs these players were with when they totaled 200-plus hits in a season.

Player	A.L. Team	N.L. Team
George Sisler	_____	_____
Al Oliver	_____	_____
Bill Buckner	_____	_____
Steve Sax	_____	_____
Vladimir Guerrero	_____	_____

B. Only five players since 1900 and through 2009 won batting titles with two different teams. Identify the clubs these players won batting titles with.

Player	Teams	
Nap Lajoie	_____	_____
Rogers Hornsby	_____	_____
Lefty O'Doul	_____	_____
Jimmie Foxx	_____	_____
Bill Madlock	_____	_____

QUIZ 13

Answers on page 93

Miscellany

1. Since 1957 when the Gold Glove award was first presented and through the 2009 season, only six players have won a Gold Glove, a league MVP Award, and a batting title in the same season. Identify any one of these six players and collect ten points.

2. Hanley Ramirez became the 13th player to win a league Rookie of the Year Award and a league batting title during his career. Collect ten points if you can name four of the other 12 players to accomplish this feat.

3. The Manager of the Year Award was first presented in 1983. Since then, only one field general has captured the honor while leading his club to a losing record. Is he Joe Girardi, Don Baylor, Lou Piniella, or Ozzie Guillen?

4. Which player holds the record for most extra base hits in a season by a switch-hitter: Mickey Mantle, Lance Berkman, Chipper Jones, or Mark Teixeira?

5. Hall of Famer Addie Joss is one of six pitchers who have thrown multiple no-hitters during their careers with one being a perfect game. Collect two points for each of the other five pitchers you can identify who have a no-hitter and a perfect game to their credit in the major leagues.

6. Only three active players have won more than one RBI crown. Collect ten points if you can identify any one of these run producers.

7. Which pitcher has the most career strikeouts (3,574) without ever leading his league in that department: Bob Gibson, Bert Blyleven, Don Sutton, or Gaylord Perry?

8. Besides Gary Sheffield, who is the only other slugger to hit 30 or more home runs in a season for five different teams: Dick Allen, Jose Canseco, Fred McGriff, or Bobby Bonds?

9. Among the 27 players with 3,000 or more hits, who is the only one to collect his 3,000th hit off a future Hall of Fame pitcher: Dave Winfield, Stan Musial, Roberto Clemente, or Robin Yount?

10. Who is the only player to steal 100 or more bases in a major league season without hitting a home run: Rickey Henderson, Maury Wills, Lou Brock, or Vince Coleman?

Here are ten questions testing your knowledge of situations involving fair or foul balls.

1. Outfielder Juan Pierre of the White Sox bunts a ball that rolls lazily up the third base line. When the ball stops dead on the foul line, half the ball is resting in fair territory while the other half is on foul ground. Fair or Foul?

Answers on page 94

2. The Padres' Everth Cabrera rips a sizzling drive that strikes the first base bag before darting into foul territory. Fair or Foul?

3. The Mariners' Chone Figgins lofts a fly down the left-field line. Scott Hairston of the A's, standing with both feet in fair territory, reaches over the foul line where he gloves the ball but drops it. Fair or Foul?

4. Ivan Rodriguez of the Nationals gets a piece of a Tim Hudson pitch and taps it foul a few feet up the third base line. The ball hits a pebble in foul territory and caroms into fair territory, where it stops rolling. Fair or Foul?

5. New York's Derek Jeter rips a Josh Beckett pitch back to the mound. The ball strikes the rubber and ricochets into the Red Sox dugout. Fair or Foul?

6. Aramis Ramirez of the Cubs hits a grounder up the third base line that bounces over the bag before landing foul about 15 feet beyond third base. Fair or Foul?

7. Texas's Josh Hamilton pokes a drive deep down the right field line at Progressive Field in Cleveland. Shin-Soo

Choo leaps above the wall in fair territory and bats the ball with his glove. The ball ends up in the seats in foul territory. Fair or Foul?

8. The Dodgers' Casey Blake lays down a bunt a few feet in front of home plate. The ball takes an unusual backspin and lands on home plate where it finally stops. Fair or Foul?

9. Adam Lind of the Blue Jays drills a shot down the right-field line at Target Field in Minnesota. The ball curves around the foul pole in foul territory and lands in the grandstand in fair territory. Fair or Foul?

10. Philadelphia's Raul Ibanez hits a high pop-fly about halfway up the first base line. The ball descends directly over the foul line. Brewers' first baseman Prince Fielder straddles the line with one foot in fair territory and the other foot on foul ground. Fielder drops the ball as Ibanez reaches first base safely. Fair or Foul?

You Make the Call . . .   *Answer on page 95*

Here's a hypothetical situation in which even a veteran umpire might go astray if he doesn't watch out.

Let's say it's the Pirates and Reds in the seventh inning of a tight battle at PNC Park in Pittsburgh. The Pirates come to bat trailing 3-1. After Bobby Crosby is retired for the first out of the inning, Garrett Jones scratches an infield hit on a slow roller between first and second. Ryan Doumit is walked, moving Jones to second.

Andrew McCutchen then sends a hopper toward shortstop Paul Janish, but Doumit edges into second just ahead of Janish's throw.

In an effort to nab McCutchen, the Reds' second baseman hurries his throw to first. A good throw would catch McCutchen, but the ball goes wild and lands in the dugout. Jones scores.

But how would you, as the umpire, place Doumit and McCutchen in order to avoid a protest game?

QUIZ 14

Answers on page 95

Miscellany

1. Twelve different players in American League history have won consecutive batting titles. Four of these 12 players accomplished the feat with the Boston Red Sox. Collect ten points if you can identify these four Red Sox batting champs.

2. Who was the last pitcher to enjoy back-to-back seasons with 25 or more victories: Juan Marichal, Denny McLain, Sandy Koufax, or Ferguson Jenkins?

3. For ten points, name the three managers with the first name of Joe who led the Yankees to a World Series title.

4. Who is the only pitcher to lead his league in wins and saves during his career: Derek Lowe, Dennis Eckersley, Kerry Wood, or John Smoltz?

5. During the 1970s the Cincinnati Reds had four different players win a National League Most Valuable Player Award, including two players with multiple honors. Collect ten points if you can name three of these MVP recipients.

6. With a .444 on-base percentage in 2009, Joe Mauer of the Twins became only the third catcher to lead the league in that category. The first to accomplish this feat was Chief Meyers for the New York Giants when he paced the N.L. with a .441 mark in 1912. Who is the only other catcher to lead his league in on-base percentage: Mickey Cochrane, Ted Simmons, Mike Piazza, or Yogi Berra?

7. Only four players in baseball history have clubbed 45 or more homers with 130-plus RBI in four consecutive seasons. If you can identify any one of these four sluggers, collect ten points.

8. The Aaron brothers combined for 2,391 RBI during their careers, with Hank totaling 2,297 and Tommy 94. What brother duo ranks second with 2,155 cumulative runs batted in: Billy and Cal Ripken, Joe and Dom DiMaggio, Lee and Carlos May, or Roberto and Sandy Alomar?

9. In 2009, Mark Teixeira became the seventh player in New York Yankees history to lead the American League in both home runs and RBI. Collect ten points if you can identify the other six Yankees to accomplish this feat.

10. Since the 1960s, many batters have struck out 150 or more times in a season, with Mark Reynolds of the Diamondbacks the first to fan 200 times in one year. Who was the first to strikeout 150 times: Mickey Mantle, Dave Nicholson, Bobby Bonds, or Reggie Jackson?

Name That Player
Answers on page 96

A. Since 1900, I am the only player to have consecutive seasons with 150 or more runs scored. In fact, I accomplished the feat twice during my career. Am I Lou Gehrig, Babe Ruth, Chuck Klein, or Ted Williams?

B. I hold the single-season mark for most RBI by a shortstop with 159. Am I Miguel Tejada, Cal Ripken, Ernie Banks, or Vern Stephens?

C. I hold the record for most times reaching base in a season through hits, bases on balls, or hit-by-pitch, with 379. Am I Barry Bonds, Babe Ruth, Ichiro Suzuki, or George Sisler?

D. Besides Robin Roberts (1951–1955), I am the only other pitcher to lead the league in innings pitched five years in a row since 1900. Am I Greg Maddux, Jim Palmer, Gaylord Perry, or Tom Seaver?

E. Ed Walsh was the first pitcher to have two seasons (1906, 1908) with ten or more shutouts. I am the only other pitcher to accomplish this feat. Am I Walter Johnson, Grover Alexander, Dean Chance, or Bob Gibson?

F. I pitched 17 seasons in the major leagues and topped my league in ERA in nine of those campaigns. Am I Roger Clemens, Sandy Koufax, Lefty Grove, or Pedro Martinez?

G. Through the 2009 season, we are the only four big-league players to have 700 or more at-bats in a single season. Two of us accomplished the feat in the American League and two of us did it in the National League. Who are we?

1. The record for most hits in a month is 68 set by Ty Cobb in July 1912. He totaled 68 hits in 127 at-bats for a .535 batting average in 30 games played.

2. Besides Lee Smith and Chad Cordero, the only other reliever to save 15 games in one month is John Wetteland, who saved 15 games for the Yankees in June 1996. He finished the year with an American League–leading 43 saves.

3. Since 1900, Hack Wilson and Joe DiMaggio hold the record for 53 RBI in one month. Wilson did it in August 1930 and DiMaggio in August 1939.

4. Sammy Sosa's record of 20 home runs in one month, set in June 1998, broke Rudy York's mark of 18 homers established in August 1937 during his rookie season in the majors with the Detroit Tigers.

5. Among pitchers since 1900, Rube Waddell set the record for most victories in one month with 10 in July 1902 as a member of the Philadelphia A's. He finished the year with a 24-7 won-lost record.

6. The 1916 New York Giants established a major league record for victories in a month when they went 29-5 in September. At the start of the month they were 56-58, 15 games behind first-place Brooklyn. At the end, after going 29-5, the Giants were 85-63 but still five games behind the Dodgers.

**Puzzle Solution
from page 10**

7. Rickey Henderson holds the record for most stolen bases in one month when he stole 33 bases in July 1983 for the Oakland A's. Henderson totaled 108 for the year.

8. Sandy Koufax never tossed five complete-game shutouts in a row during his career. Bob Gibson did it in June 1968, Don Drysdale in May 1968, and Orel Hershiser in September 1988.

9. Johnny Vander Meer is the only pitcher to throw two no-hitters in one month when he tossed back-to-back hitless games on June 11 and June 15, 1938.

10. Nolan Ryan holds the record for most strikeouts by a pitcher in one month—he fanned 87 batters in June 1977 and finished the year with 341.

They Said It

• "Baseball hasn't forgotten me. I go to a lot of old-timers games and I haven't lost a thing. I sit in the bullpen and let people throw things at me. Just like old times."
—Former catcher Bob Uecker

• "Baseball must be a great game to survive the fools who run *it.*" *—Hall of Famer Bill Terry*

• A baseball game is simply a nervous breakdown divided into nine innings. *—Former pitcher Earl Wilson*

• "There are three types of baseball players: those who make it happen, those who watch it happen, and those who wonder what happens."
—Former manager Tommy Lasorda

• "I think about baseball when I wake up in the morning. I think about it all day and I dream about it at night. The only time I don't think about it is when I'm playing it."
—Hall of Famer Carl Yastrzemski

• "Finish last in your league and they call you Idiot. Finish last in medical school and they call you Doctor."
—Abe Lemons

• "I knew when my career was over. In 1965 my baseball card came out with no picture." *—Bob Uecker*

ANSWERS TO QUIZ 2 *From page 12*

1. The seven players to win five or more home run titles from 1900 through 2009 are Babe Ruth, 12 (1918–1921, 1923–1924, 1926–1931); Mike Schmidt, 8 (1974–1976, 1980–1981, 1983–1984, 1986); Ralph Kiner, 7 (1946–1952); Gavvy Cravath, 6 (1913–1915, 1917–1919); Mel Ott, 6 (1932, 1934, 1936–1938, 1942); Harmon Killebrew, 6 (1959, 1962–1964, 1967, 1969); and Alex Rodriguez, 5 (2001–2003, 2005, 2007).

2. The four players with the last name "Williams" who have won a league home run crown include Cy Williams (1916, 1929, 1923, 1927), Ken Williams (1922), Ted Williams (1941–1942, 1947, 1949), and Matt Williams (1994).

3. Besides Sam Crawford and Mark McGwire, the other player to win a home run title in both the American and National leagues is Fred McGriff. Crawford won the N.L. title in 1901 with the Reds and the A.L. crown in 1908 with the Tigers. McGwire captured titles in 1987 and 1996 in the A.L. with the A's and in 1998–1999 in the N.L. with the Cardinals. McGriff led the A.L. in homers in 1989 with the Blue Jays and in the N.L. in 1992 with the Padres.

4. Mike Piazza never led the league in home runs during his career. The Mets' league home run champions include Darryl Strawberry (1988), Howard Johnson (1991), and Dave Kingman (1982).

5. Although he hit the most career home runs by a second baseman, Jeff Kent never captured a home run title during his career. Bobby Grich tied for the A.L. lead in 1981, Ryne Sandberg topped the N.L. in 1990, and Rogers Hornsby led the senior circuit in 1922 and 1925.

6. The five switch-hitters to win a league home run title include Ripper Collins (1934), Mickey Mantle (1955–1956, 1958, 1960), Howard Johnson (1991), Eddie Murray (1981), and Mark Teixeira (2009).

7. The last National League player to win three consecutive home run titles was Mike Schmidt when he paced the league from 1974 through 1976 with the Philadelphia Phillies.

8. Besides Dick Allen's home run crowns in 1972 and 1974, the only other White Sox slugger to pace the A.L. in homers was Bill Melton with 33 in 1971.

9. The 13 Boston Red Sox to win an A.L. home run crown from 1901 through 2009 include Buck Freeman (1903), Jake Stahl (1910), Tris Speaker (1912), Babe Ruth (1918–1919), Jimmie Foxx (1939), Ted Williams (1941–1942, 1947, 1949), Tony Conigliaro (1965), Carl Yastrzemski (1967), Jim Rice (1977–1978, 1983), Dwight Evans (1981), Tony Armas (1984), Manny Ramirez (2004), and David Ortiz (2006).

10. True. Rafael Palmeiro has the most career home runs to his credit without ever capturing a season home run title.

Most Career HR Without a Season Title

+Totals through 2009

Player	Career HR	Season High
Rafael Palmeiro	569	47
Frank Thomas	521	43
Gary Sheffield	509	43
Stan Musial	475	39
Carlos Delgado+	473	44
Dave Winfield	465	37
Jeff Bagwell	449	47
Cal Ripken	431	34
Mike Piazza	427	40
Chipper Jones+	426	45
Billy Williams	426	42
Jason Giambi+	409	43
Vladimir Guerrero+	407	44
Al Kaline	399	29
Joe Carter	396	35
Harold Baines	384	29
Jim Edmonds+	382	42
Tony Perez	379	40
Norm Cash	377	41
Jeff Kent	377	37

Player	Career HR	Season High
Carlton Fisk	376	37
Gil Hodges	370	42
Gary Gaetti	360	35
Yogi Berra	358	30
Greg Vaughn	355	50
Luis Gonzalez	354	57
Lee May	354	39
Ellis Burks	352	40
Chili Davis	350	30

BASEBALL BY THE RULES 1 ANSWERS

From page 13

1. False. Rule 3.15: the interference must be intentional.

2. False. Rule 7.11: the coach shall vacate space needed by a fielder who is attempting to field a batted or thrown ball.

3. True. Rule 3.15: the coach did not intentionally interfere with the defensive team making a play.

4. True. Rule 3.15: in this case the interference was intentional.

5. False. Rule 4.06 (a-3): a coach cannot call "Time" for the obvious purpose of trying to make the pitcher balk.

6. True. Rule 7.09 (g): because Figgins intentionally interfered to break up a double play, Ichiro (the runner closest to home plate) is also called out.

7. False. Rule 6.06 (a): if a batter hits a ball fair or foul with one or both feet on the ground entirely out of the batter's box, he shall be called out.

8. True. Rule 4.09 (a) and 7.10 (b): a run does not score if the third out is made by a preceding runner who failed to touch a base.

9. False. Rule 6.05 (b): if a foul tip first strikes the catcher's glove or hand and then goes on through and is caught by both hands against the body or protector before the ball touches the ground, it is a legal catch and is a strike.

10. False. Rule 5.09 (b): runners may not advance when the plate umpire interferes with the catcher's throw.

DID YOU KNOW. . . that there have been 17 major league games in which pitchers from opposing teams hit home runs against each other? It has been accomplished ten times since 1900, including:

Case Patten, Senators / Clark Griffith, White Sox	August 20, 1901
Milt Gaston, Browns / Ted Blankenship, White Sox	April 18, 1927
Cliff Chambers, Pirates / Ralph Branca, Dodgers	June 8, 1950
Don Larsen, Yankees / Dick Brodowski, Red Sox	August 16, 1955
Pedro Ramos, Twins / Eli Grba, Angels	May 12, 1961
Buster Narum, Senators / Earl Wilson, Red Sox	September 14, 1965
Ray Sadecki, Giants / Tony Cloninger, Braves	July 3, 1966
Kevin Gross, Expos / Fernando Valenzuela, Dodgers	May 14, 1990
Marvin Freeman, Rockies / Kevin Foster, Cubs	May 23, 1995
Denny Stark, Rockies / Kevin Millwood, Braves	May 18, 2002

ANSWERS TO QUIZ 3 *From page 15*

1. During the decade of the 2000s (2000–2009), Alex Rodriguez hit the most home runs in the major leagues with 435. Barry Bonds hit 317, Manny Ramirez 348, and Albert Pujols 366.

2. Ichiro Suzuki topped all hitters during 2000–2009 with 2,030 hits, followed by Derek Jeter at 1,940. Michael Young had 1,662 and Todd Helton 1,756.

3. The most victories by a pitcher during the decade was 148 by Andy Pettitte. Randy Johnson had 143, Curt Schilling 117, and Greg Maddux 134.

4. The closer who registered the most saves during the 2000s with 397 was Mariano Rivera of the Yankees. Trevor Hoffman saved 363, Billy Wagner 284, Francisco Rodriguez 243, and Roberto Hernandez 90.

5. With 95 triples, Jimmy Rollins led all major league hitters during the 2000-2009 decade. Johnny Damon hit 58, Carl Crawford 92, and Juan Pierre 79.

6. With a minimum of 4,000 plate appearances during the 2000s, the leading hitter in the majors was Albert Pujols with a .334 batting average. Ichiro Suzuki posted a .333 mark, Todd Helton .331, and Matt Holliday .318.

7. The pitcher who completed the most shutouts during the decade was Roy Halladay with 14. Johan Santana tossed six, Tom Glavine seven, and Roger Clemens one.

8. The New York Yankees won the most games from 2000 through 2009 with 965 victories. The Boston Red Sox won 920 during that span, the St. Louis Cardinals 913, Los Angeles Angels 901, and Atlanta Braves 892.

9. The only pitcher to throw two no-hit games during the 2000s was Chicago White Sox left-hander Mark Buehrle. He no-hit the Texas Rangers on April 18, 2007, at U.S. Cellular Field and at the same location on July 23, 2009, Buehrle tossed a perfect game against the Tampa Bay Rays.

10. The manager who was credited with the most victories during the 2000s was Joe Torre with 952 wins—773 with the New York Yankees and 179 with the Los Angeles Dodgers.

ANSWERS TO PHOTO QUIZ 1

From page 16

1. The Hall of Fame sluggers are Duke Snider, left, and Ernie Banks. Snider won a home run title for the Dodgers in

1956 with 43 while Banks captured N.L. home run crowns with the Cubs in 1958 and 1960.

2. The pictured 1959 American League home run champ is Rocky Colavito. With the Cleveland Indians, Colavito tied for the HR crown with Washington Senators slugger Harmon Killebrew, each player totaling 42.

3. The Dodgers infield, pictured left to right, is third baseman Ron Cey, shortstop Bill Russell, second baseman Davey Lopes, and first baseman Steve Garvey. The four played together as a unit from 1973 through 1981. The first game they started together in 1973 was on June 13 against the Phillies; their last was Game 6 of the 1981 World Series on October 28 versus the New York Yankees.

4. The two Braves pitchers are Warren Spahn, left, and Johnny Sain. The two pitched together as teammates from 1942, 1946–1951 when they combined to win 207 games for the Boston Braves.

5. The well-known pitching coach is Dave Duncan, who was a catcher in the major leagues for 11 seasons with the Kansas City/Oakland A's (1964, 1967–1972), Cleveland Indians (1973–1974), and Baltimore Orioles (1975–1976). He began his coaching career in 1978 with the Indians and then the Seattle Mariners in 1982 before being manager Tony La Russa's pitching coach since 1983 with the Chicago White Sox, Oakland A's, and St. Louis Cardinals.

DID YOU KNOW . . . that Dave Duncan has coached seven different 20-game winners and four Cy Young Award winners during his reign as a major league pitching coach? The 20-game winners under his supervision include LaMarr Hoyt and Richard Dotson (White Sox), Dave Stewart and Bob Welch (A's), and Darryl Kile, Matt Morris, and Chris Carpenter (Cardinals). The Cy Young winners include Hoyt (1983), Welch (1990), Dennis Eckersley (1992), and Carpenter (2005).

1. 1973 Atlanta Braves, Davey Johnson
1996 Colorado Rockies, Ellis Burks
1997 Colorado Rockies, Larry Walker

2. The four American League players to tie for the league lead in home runs with 22 in the strike-interrupted 1981 campaign were Tony Armas, Oakland A's; Eddie Murray, Baltimore Orioles; Bobby Grich, California Angels; and Dwight Evans, Boston Red Sox.

3. The ten pitchers to win 25 or more games in a season from 1968 through 2009 are:

Year	Wins	Pitcher, Team
1968	31	Denny McLain, Detroit Tigers
	26	Juan Marichal, San Francisco Giants
1969	25	Tom Seaver, New York Mets
1971	25	Mickey Lolich, Detroit Tigers
1972	27	Steve Carlton, Philadelphia Phillies
1974	25	Jim Hunter, Oakland A's
	25	Ferguson Jenkins, Texas Rangers
1978	25	Ron Guidry, New York Yankees
1980	25	Steve Stone, Baltimore Orioles
1990	27	Bob Welch, Oakland A's

Note: Among these ten 25-plus game winners, seven captured the Cy Young Award. The three who did not were Ferguson Jenkins, who finished second in the voting to Hunter in 1974; Mickey Lolich, who placed second to Vida Blue of the A's (who went 24-8 with a 1.82 ERA and 301 strikeouts) in 1971; and Juan Marichal, who didn't receive a single vote in 1968 when Bob Gibson of the Cardinals was a unanimous selection for N.L. Cy Young honors with a 22-9 record, 1.12 ERA, and 13 shutouts.

ANSWERS TO QUIZ 4 *From page 18*

1. The youngest pitcher to win a Cy Young Award is Dwight Gooden, who was 20 years, 326 days old at the end of the 1985 season when he captured top pitching honors in the N.L. with the Mets after going 24-4 with a 1.53 ERA and 268 strikeouts. Fernando Valenzuela was 20 years, 337 days old when he won the 1981 Cy Young. Bret Saberhagen was 21 when he won the A.L. Cy Young Award in 1985, and Tim Lincecum was 24 when he won his first award in 2008.

Sandy Koufax

2. Roger Clemens is the only pitcher to win a Cy Young Award at age 40; he won N.L. honors in 2004 with Houston at age 41. Gaylord Perry was 39 when he captured the award in 1978 with the Padres; Early Wynn was 39 when he was the A.L. Cy Young recipient with the White Sox in 1959; and Warren Spahn was 36 when he won the award in 1957.

3. The nine pitchers to win a Cy Young and MVP Award in the same season are Don Newcombe (1956), Sandy Koufax (1963), Denny McLain and Bob Gibson (1968), Vida Blue (1971), Rollie Fingers (1981), Willie Hernandez (1984), Roger Clemens (1986), and Dennis Eckersley (1992).

4. In 1965, Sandy Koufax of the Los Angeles Dodgers became the only pitcher to throw a perfect game in the same season he captured Cy Young Award honors. He went 25-8 with a 2.04 ERA and 382 strikeouts while pitching a perfect game against the Cubs on September 9.

5. The three pitchers to win the Cy Young Award as members of the Toronto Blue Jays include Pat Hentgen (1996), Roger Clemens (1997, 1998), and Roy Halladay (2003).

6. Besides Sandy Koufax, the five other pitchers to win a Cy Young Award and strike out 300 or more batters in the same season are Vida Blue (1971), Steve Carlton (1972),

Mike Scott (1986), Randy Johnson (1999–2002), and Pedro Martinez (1997, 1999).

7. In 1974, Mike Marshall of the Dodgers became the first relief pitcher to win the Cy Young Award when he went 15-12 with a league-leading 21 saves and a record 106 appearances.

8. The four American League Cy Young Award winners from 1967 through 1976 whose first name was "Jim" were Jim Lonborg, Red Sox (1967), Jim Perry, Twins (1970), Jim Palmer, Orioles (1973, 1975–1976), and Jim Hunter, Yankees (1975).

9. The first pitcher to win the Cy Young Award without benefit of a 20-win season was Tom Seaver in 1973 when he won the N.L. honor with the Mets by going 19-10 while leading the league with a 2.08 ERA and 251 strikeouts.

10. The 15 pitchers to win multiple Cy Young Awards in the majors are Sandy Koufax (1963, 1965–1966), Bob Gibson (1968, 1970), Denny McLain (1968–1969), Steve Carlton (1972, 1977, 1980, 1982), Gaylord Perry (1972, 1978), Jim Palmer (1973, 1975–1976), Tom Seaver (1969, 1973, 1975), Roger Clemens (1986–1987, 1991, 1997–1998, 2001, 2004), Bret Saberhagen (1985, 1989), Greg Maddux (1992–1995), Tom Glavine (1991, 1998), Randy Johnson (1995, 1999–2002), Pedro Martinez (1997, 1999–2000), Johan Santana (2004, 2006) and Tim Lincecum (2008–2009).

Name That Hall of Famer

From page 20

1. Bob Feller. During his career with the Cleveland Indians, the right-handed Hall of Famer wore uniform No. 19

and led the American League in victories in 1939 (24), 1940 (27), 1941 (25), 1946 (26), 1947 (20), and 1951 (22). In his first major league start on August 23, 1936, at age 17, he pitched nine innings and allowed six hits and four walks while fanning 15 St. Louis Browns' batters.

2. Robin Yount. During his 20 seasons in the majors, all with the Milwaukee Brewers, Yount won fielding titles as a shortstop in 1981 and as a center fielder in 1986, 1988, and 1993. He won the American League MVP Award in 1982 and 1989.

Most Strikeouts, Relief Pitcher, Game

Pitcher, Team	Date	IP	SO
Randy Johnson, D'backs	July 18, 2001	7.0	16
Walter Johnson, Senators	July 25, 1913	11.1	15
Rube Marquard, Giants	May 13, 1911	8.0	14
Denny McLain, Tigers	June 15, 1965	6.2	14
Billy O'Dell, Giants	July 4, 1961	9.0	13
Rube Waddell, A's	August 18, 1905	7.1	12
Walter Brown, Yankees	June 3, 1933	6.1	12
Diego Segui, Red Sox	Sept. 22, 1974	7.2	12
Steve Hamilton, Yankees	May 11, 1963	8.1	11
Dick Radatz, Red Sox	June 11, 1963	8.2	11
Sonny Siebert, Indians	May 10, 1964	6.0	11
Moe Drabowsky, Orioles*	Oct. 5, 1966	6.2	11
Jim Ray, Astros	April 15, 1968	7.0	11

* World Series

ANSWERS TO QUIZ 5 *From page 21*

1. The nine players with multiple 50-homer seasons include Babe Ruth (1920–1921, 1927–1928), Jimmie Foxx (1932, 1938), Ralph Kiner (1947, 1949), Willie Mays (1955, 1965), Mickey Mantle (1956, 1961), Mark McGwire (1996–1999), Sammy Sosa (1998–2001), Ken Griffey, Jr. (1997–1998), and Alex Rodriguez (2001–2002, 2007).

2. Hack Wilson was the second player after Babe Ruth to club 50 or more home runs in a season when he hit 56 for the Chicago Cubs in 1930.

3. Tom Gordon surrendered home runs to Cecil Fielder in 1990 and to his son Prince in 2007 during their 50-HR campaigns. Cecil Fielder hit his 28th of 51 homers in 1990 off Gordon on July 6 when Gordon pitched for Kansas City. Prince clubbed No. 32 of his 50 homers off Gordon and the Phillies on August 4, 2007.

4. Barry Bonds was the oldest player to hit 50 or more home runs in a season. He was 36 years old during his record-setting 73-homer season in 2001 for the San Francisco Giants.

5. The three players to have a 50-homer season with different teams are Jimmie Foxx, Mark McGwire, and Alex Rodriguez. Foxx hit 58 with the A's in 1932 and 50 with the Red Sox in 1938. McGwire hit 52 with the A's in 1996 and 70 and 65 with the Cardinals in 1998 and 1999 respectively. McGwire also hit 58 in 1997 while splitting the season with the A's and Cardinals. Rodriguez reached the 50-homer plateau with the Rangers in 2001–2002 and with the Yankees in 2007.

6. The lowest slugging percentage in a season for a player who hit 50 or more home runs is .575 by Andruw Jones of the Braves in 2005 when he hit 51 homers. The other two players with 50 homers and a slugging percentage below .600 are Cecil Fielder of the Tigers in 1990 (51 homers, .592) and Greg Vaughn of the Padres in 1998 (50 HR, .597).

7. The fastest player to reach the 50-homer mark was Barry Bonds in 2001. He hit his 50th homer on August 11 and ended the year with 73.

8. Besides Jimmie Foxx, the only other player to win a league batting title and hit 50 homers in the same season is Mickey Mantle in 1956, when he led the American League with 52 homers and a .353 batting average.

9. In 1997, when Mark McGwire hit 58 homers with the A's and Cardinals, he scored only 87 runs. The only other player to hit 50 homers in a season without scoring 100 runs is Andruw Jones, who scored 95 runs in 2005 when he hit 51 homers with the Braves.

10. The two players to hit 50 or more homers in a season with the Cleveland Indians are Albert Belle and Jim Thome. Belle slugged 50 for the Indians in 1995, and Thome hit 52 for the Tribe in 2002.

DID YOU KNOW . . . the Yankees have the most players who have hit 50 homers in a season with four? The Giants have had three, and the Cubs, Athletics, Tigers, and Indians have had two players each.

BASEBALL BY THE RULES 2 ANSWERS *From page 22*

1. False. The fielder must secure possession after making immediate contact with the ground.

2. True. The fielder receives credit for a catch if he drops the ball while in the act of transferring it after he has had control and secure possession of the ball.

3. False. If the ball deflects off an outfielder's glove and over the fence in fair territory, it is ruled a home run.

4. True. It is a legal catch if a batted ball caroms off the body of one fielder and is caught by another as long as the ball doesn't touch the ground, an umpire, a wall, or some object other than the fielder.

5. True. For a catch to be legal after a player falls to the ground unconscious and has the ball, a teammate must remove the ball from the fallen player's glove.

6. True. If a ball becomes lodged in a fielder's glove and that fielder throws his glove with the ball in it to the first baseman before the runner reaches the bag, the first baseman gets credit for a legal catch and the batter-runner is called out.

7. False. The first baseman must show the ball is secure in his glove or hand for a legal catch.

8. True. The fielder should receive credit for a catch even if his momentum carries him into a dugout and he receives assistance to prevent him from falling.

9. True. A fielder is allowed to make a catch, carry the ball into the dugout, and make a throw as long as he remains on his feet.

10. True. Runners should be awarded two bases if a fielder makes a throw from the dugout and the ball slips out of his hand and drops to the floor of the dugout while making the throw.

11. False. On catcher's interference calls, the ball remains alive.

12. False. When an outfielder falls into the stands after making a catch, the ball is dead but runners are awarded only one base.

13. False. The runners can advance at their own risk. The ball is not dead.

14. False. The Infield Fly Rule can be called even when an outfielder comes charging in, on a windy day for instance, to make a catch in the general infield area.

15. False. Bunts are not included in the Infield Fly Rule.

ANSWERS TO QUIZ 6   *From page 24*

1. From 1917 through 2009, the only two pitchers to win and lose 20 games in the same season in the major leagues are Wilbur Wood and Phil Niekro. Wood went 24-20 for the White Sox in 1973, and Niekro posted a 21-20 mark for the Braves in 1979.

2. Bobo Newsom registered the highest ERA for a 20-game winner when he went 20-16 in 1938 for the St. Louis Browns with a 5.08 ERA. Ray Kremer is the only other pitcher to have an ERA over 5.00 while winning 20 games; he was 20-12 for the Pirates in 1930 with a 5.02 ERA.

3. The highest winning percentage for a 20-game winner is .893 by Ron Guidry of the Yankees when he recorded a 25-3 mark in 1978.

4. Besides Christy Mathewson, the only other major league pitcher since 1900 to win 20 or more games in a season 13 times is Warren Spahn. The Hall of Fame left-hander was a 20-game winner for the Braves in 1947, 1949–1951, 1953–1954, 1956–1961, and 1963.

5. From 1903 through 1914, Christy Mathewson of the New York Giants set a major league record for consecutive 20-win seasons with 12. During that span he had a combined 327-133 won-lost record for a .711 winning percentage.

6. The four pitchers to win 20 or more games in a season for three different teams since 1900 are Gaylord Perry (Giants, Indians, Padres), Roger Clemens (Red Sox, Blue Jays, Yankees), Grover Alexander (Phillies, Cubs, Cardinals), and Carl Mays (Red Sox, Yankees, Reds).

7. Besides Claude Osteen, the 10 other 20-game winners for the Dodgers since 1958 when they moved to Los Angeles include Sandy Koufax, Don Drysdale, Bill Singer, Al Downing, Andy Messersmith, Don Sutton, Tommy John, Fernando Valenzuela, Orel Hershiser, and Ramon Martinez.

8. True. David Cone is the only pitcher to have a 20-win season for both the Yankees and Mets. He went 20-3 for the Mets in 1988 and 20-7 for the Yankees in 1998.

9. Rick Sutcliffe is the only pitcher to win 20 games in a season while splitting the year with two different teams and winning the Cy Young Award. In 1984 he went 20-6, starting the season with the Cleveland Indians and posting a 4-5 won-lost record before being traded to the Cubs and going 16-1 to earn the National League Cy Award.

10. Dennis Martinez holds the major league record for

Puzzle Solution from page 25

most career victories without a 20-win season. During his career, Martinez won 245 games with a single-season high of 16 victories in 1978, 1982, 1989, and 1992.

Team Identification Answers
From page 26

Listed are the teams these players played their first major league game for.

Player, Team	Player, Team
Ryne Sandberg, **Phillies**	Curt Schilling, **Orioles**
Joe Torre, **Braves**	Juan Pierre, **Rockies**
Derrek Lee, **Padres**	Trevor Hoffman, **Marlins**
Roberto Alomar, **Padres**	Johnny Damon, **Royals**
Jeff Kent, **Blue Jays**	Joe Carter, **Cubs**
Gaylord Perry, **Giants**	Orlando Cabrera, **Expos**
Sammy Sosa, **Rangers**	Scott Rolen, **Phillies**
Willie Randolph, **Pirates**	Bobby Bonilla, **White Sox**
Reggie Jackson, **A's**	Gary Sheffield, **Brewers**

ANSWERS TO QUIZ 7 *From page 27*

1. False. Besides Reggie Jackson, Babe Ruth hit three homers in one World Series game twice during his career: Game 4, October 6, 1926, against the St. Louis Cardinals, and Game 4, October 9, 1928, against the Cardinals.

2. False. On October 13, 1969, Jim Palmer pitched the only no-hitter of his big league career against the Oakland A's at Memorial Stadium in Baltimore.

3. True. Through 2009, the most strikeouts in a season for Albert Pujols occurred in 2001 when he was a rookie with the Cardinals and fanned 93 times.

4. True. Eric Gagne is the only closer, through 2009, to save 50 games in a season without blowing a single opportunity. In 2003 he saved a league-leading 55 games for the Dodgers with no blown saves.

5. False. Hank Aaron won only four N.L. home run titles. Mike Schmidt won eight home run crowns, the most in N.L. history.

6. True. When elected to the Hall of Fame, Sandy Koufax received 87 percent of the vote, appearing on 344 of 396 ballots.

7. False. Besides Ted Williams, Rogers Hornsby also won two Triple Crowns when he led the N.L. in homers, RBI, and batting average in 1922 and 1925 for the Cardinals. Williams accomplished the feat for the Red Sox in 1942 and 1947.

8. True. Since 1900 no player has scored more career runs without leading his league in runs scored than Tris Speaker's total of 1,882.

9. False. In 1974, Pete Rose finished with a single-season high of 106 walks for the Cincinnati Reds.

10. False. Jim Bunning finished his career after the 1971 season with 2,855 lifetime strikeouts. At the time of his retirement, Bunning was second on the all-time strikeout list behind Walter Johnson's 3,509. Bob Gibson became the second pitcher to fan 3,000 batters on July 17, 1974.

11. False. Besides Babe Ruth and Lou Gehrig, the other two teammates to drive in 150 or more runs in the same season are Jimmie Foxx and Al Simmons of the 1930 and 1932 Philadelphia A's, and Ted Williams and Vern Stephens of the 1949 Boston Red Sox. Ruth and Gehrig did it with the Yankees in 1927, 1930, and 1931.

12. True. At age 23 years, 139 days on September 25, 2007, Prince Fielder of the Brewers became the youngest player in major league history to club 50 homers in a season.

13. True. Randy Johnson is the only pitcher to strikeout 2,000 or more batters with two teams. For the Seattle Mariners he fanned a career total 2,162 batters, and for the Arizona Diamondbacks he struck out 2,077.

14. True. During Rickey Henderson's record-setting season of 1982 with 130 stolen bases, he also set the mark for most times caught attempting to steal with 42.

15. True. Tony La Russa is the only manger to be credited with 1,000 or more victories in both leagues. Through 2009 he had 1,320 in the A.L. and 1,232 in the N.L.

16. False. On June 17, 2009, Ivan Rodriguez broke Carlton Fisk's record of 2,226 games caught.

17. True. In 1968, Randy Hundley caught 160 of the Chicago Cubs' 162 games, starting 156 of those contests and playing every inning in 146.

18. False. There are three 300-game winners since 1900 who never led their league in victories—Don Sutton, Eddie Plank, and Nolan Ryan.

19. True. Among the ten managers with 2,000 or more career wins, Joe Torre is the only one to win a league MVP Award during his active days as a player. In 1971 with the Cardinals, Torre won MVP honors by leading the N.L. with 230 hits, a .363 batting average, and 137 RBI.

20. False. Ryan Howard and Bobby Bonds are the only players to strike out 180 or more times in a season while maintaining a .300 batting average. In 1970, Bonds hit .302 with 189 strikeouts for the Giants. In 2006, Howard whiffed 181 times while hitting at a .313 clip for the Phillies.

21. False. Ted Williams won two A.L. MVP Awards with the Boston Red Sox, 1946 and 1949.

22. True. Mitch Williams surrendered the home run to Joe Carter that won the 1993 World Series for the Toronto Blue Jays over the Philadelphia Phillies. Carter hit a walk-off three-run homer to win the game, 8-6, and the Series, 4-2.

23. False. Besides his record-setting 61-homer season in 1961, Roger Maris also hit 30 or more homers in a single campaign in 1960 when he clubbed 39 and in 1962 when he hit 33.

24. True. Ichiro Suzuki is the only player to hit an inside-the-park-home run in an All-Star Game (through 2009) when he did it in the fifth inning in 2007 off Padres pitcher Chris Young at AT&T Park in San Francisco.

25. False. During his career, which consisted of 310 lifetime saves, Rich Gossage recorded 30 or more saves in a season twice. He saved 33 games in 1980 and 30 in 1982 for the New York Yankees.

BASEBALL BY THE RULES 3 ANSWERS

From page 29

1. True. Rule 3.05 (a): The pitcher named in the batting order shall pitch to the first batter or any substitute batter until such batter is put out or reaches first base, unless the pitcher sustains injury or illness which, in the judgment of the umpire-in-chief, incapacitates him from pitching.

2. True. Rule 4.11 (c): If the home team scores the winning run in its half of the ninth inning (or its half of an extra inning after a tie), the game ends immediately when the winning run is scored.

3. False. Rule 7.09 (m): If in the judgment of the umpire, the runner deliberately and intentionally kicks a batted ball on which the infielder has missed a play, then the runner shall be called out for interference.

4. False. Rule 7.09 (m): The runner is out and the ball is dead. Give Cabrera first base.

5. True. Rule 7.10 (b): Any runner should be called out on appeal when with the ball in play, while advancing or returning to a base, he fails to touch each base in order before he, or a missed base, is tagged. When the ball is dead, no runner may return to touch a missed base or one he has left after he has advanced to and touched a base beyond the missed base.

6. False. Rule 7.09 (f): It is interference by a batter or a runner when any batter or runner who has just been put out hinders or impedes any following play being made on a runner. Such runner shall be declared out for the interference of his teammate. If the batter or a runner continues to advance after he has been put out, he shall not by that act alone be considered as confusing, hindering, or impeding the fielders.

7. False. Rule 5.02: Should a ball come partially apart in a game, it is in play until the play is completed.

8. True. Rule 8.05 (m): If there is a runner or runners on base, it is a balk when the pitcher delivers the pitch from the set position without coming to a stop.

9. False. Rule 2.00: A fair ball is a batted ball that settles on fair ground between home and first base, or between home and third base, or that is on or over fair territory when bounding to the outfield past first or third base, or that touches first, second or third base, or that first falls on fair territory on or beyond first base or third base, or that, while on or over fair territory touches the person of an umpire or player, or that, while over fair territory, passes out of the playing field in flight. A fair fly shall be judged according to the relative position of the ball and the foul line, including the foul pole, and not as to whether the fielder is on fair or foul territory at the time he touches the ball.

10. False. Rule 6.08 (b): The batter becomes a runner and is entitled to first base without liability to be put out when he (or his uniform) is touched by a pitched ball which he is not attempting to hit unless (1) the ball is in the strike zone when it touches the batter, or (2) the batter makes no attempt to avoid being touched by the ball. If the ball is in the strike zone when it touches the batter, it shall be called a strike, whether or not the batter tries to avoid the ball. If the ball is outside the strike zone when it touches the batter, it shall be called a ball if he makes no attempt to avoid being touched.

Fill in the Blank Answers
From page 31

A. Besides No. 42, which is retired by all major league clubs in honor of Jackie Robinson, here are the Yankees' retired uniform numbers through 2009.

Billy Martin	No. 1	Joe DiMaggio	No. 5
Babe Ruth	No. 3	Mickey Mantle	No. 7
Lou Gehrig	No. 4	Bill Dickey	No. 8

Yogi Berra	No. 8	Don Mattingly	No. 23
Roger Maris	No. 9	Elston Howard	No. 32
Phil Rizzuto	No. 10	Casey Stengel	No. 37
Thurman Munson	No. 15	Reggie Jackson	No. 44
Whitey Ford	No. 16	Ron Guidry	No. 49

B. Here are the eight major league players with 3,000 hits and 400 home runs.

Hank Aaron	755 home runs	3,771 hits
Willie Mays	660 home runs	3,283 hits
Rafael Palmeiro	569 home runs	3,020 hits
Eddie Murray	504 home runs	3,255 hits
Stan Musial	475 home runs	3,630 hits
Dave Winfield	465 home runs	3,110 hits
Carl Yastrzemski	452 home runs	3,419 hits
Cal Ripken, Jr.	431 home runs	3,184 hits

ANSWERS TO PHOTO QUIZ 2

From page 32

A. Ron Guidry	H. Tom Glavine	N. John Wetteland
B. Frank Howard	I. Sparky Lyle	O. Dave Kingman
C. Jim Palmer	J. Lou Gehrig	P. Eddie Mathews
D. Ted Williams	K. Magglio	Q. Luis Gonzalez
E. Ted Kluszewski	Ordonez	R. Sammy Sosa
F. Kirby Puckett	L. Johnny Damon	S. A. J. Burnett
G. Dick Williams	M. Paul Konerko	T. Jim Edmonds

ANSWERS TO QUIZ 8   *From page 33*

1. The ten players who have won three league MVP Awards from 1931 through 2009 include Jimmie Foxx (1932–1933, 1938), Joe DiMaggio (1939, 1941, 1947), Stan Musial (1943, 1946, 1948), Roy Campanella (1951, 1953, 1955), Yogi Berra (1951, 1954–1955), Mickey Mantle (1956–1957, 1962), Mike Schmidt (1980–1981, 1986), Barry Bonds

(1990, 1992–1993, 2001–2004), Alex Rodriguez (2003, 2005, 2007), and Albert Pujols (2005, 2008–2009).

2. The 15 players who have won the MVP through unanimous selection are Hank Greenberg (1935), Al Rosen (1953), Mickey Mantle (1956), Frank Robinson (1966), Denny McLain (1968), Reggie Jackson (1973), Jose Canseco (1988), Frank Thomas (1993), and Ken Griffey (1997) in the American League. In the National League they are Orlando Cepeda (1967), Mike Schmidt (1980), Jeff Bagwell (1994), Ken Caminiti (1996), Barry Bonds (2002), and Albert Pujols (2009).

Albert Pujols

3. Hall of Famer Eddie Murray never won a league MVP Award during his 21 seasons in the majors. He finished second in the voting in 1982 and 1983.

4. Besides Carl Hubbell, the only other pitcher to win multiple MVP Awards is Hal Newhouser, who won the honor in consecutive seasons with the Tigers in 1944–1945.

5. The nine different A.L. MVP winners from the Boston Red Sox include Jimmie Foxx (1938), Ted Williams (1946, 1949), Jackie Jensen (1958), Carl Yastrzemski (1967), Fred Lynn (1975), Jim Rice (1978), Roger Clemens (1986), Mo Vaughn (1995), and Dustin Pedroia (2008).

6. The first player to win consecutive MVP Awards was Jimmie Foxx in 1932–1933 with the Philadelphia A's.

7. Excluding pitchers, the nine MVP winners who were switch-hitters were Jimmy Rollins (2007), Chipper Jones (1999), Ken Caminiti (1996), Terry Pendleton (1991), Willie McGee (1985), Pete Rose (1973), Maury Wills (1962), Mickey Mantle (1956–1957, 1962), and Frankie Frisch (1931).

8. In 1950 the Phillies' Jim Konstanty became the first relief pitcher to win a league MVP Award when he went 16-7 in 74 games with a 2.66 ERA, helping his club to the N.L. pennant.

9. The two players to capture Rookie of the Year honors and the league MVP Award in the same season are Fred Lynn of the Red Sox in 1975 and Ichiro Suzuki of the Mariners in 2001.

10. Before Joe Mauer of the Twins in 2009, the last catcher to win a league Most Valuable Player Award was Ivan Rodriguez of the Texas Rangers in 1999.

ANSWERS TO QUIZ 9

From page 34

1. Steve Garvey
2. Mike Piazza
3. Curt Schilling
4. Omar Vizquel
5. Larry Walker
6. Fred McGriff
7. Manny Ramirez
8. Craig Biggio
9. Bert Blyleven
10. George Scott

Omar Vizquel

BASEBALL BY THE RULES 4 ANSWERS

From page 36

1. No. Appeals on half-swings may be made only when a "ball" has been called. Credit Carpenter with a strikeout.

2. None. The third out was made by the batter-runner before he touched first base.

3. No. This is a foul ball since the ball rolled foul before reaching or passing third base.

4. There's no need for a substitute runner because Shin-Soo Choo would be called out because of the third base coach's interference.

5. Vernon Wells is out on strike three and is unable to go to first because first base is occupied with less than two outs.

6. No. Since it was clearly not Shane Victorino's intention to bunt the wild pitch, this is a foul ball.

7. No. Felix Hernandez's no-hitter is no longer intact. Credit J. D. Drew with a base hit.

8. Yes. An offering from a pitcher to a batter that bounces on its way toward the plate can be hit by the hitter.

9. Yes. A. J. Burnett is guilty of obstruction because he is not fielding a ball in flight near him.

10. No. Chris Coghlan has a right to run there. Hanley Ramirez's run counts since Coghlan did not intentionally interfere with Todd Helton's throw.

You Make the Call Answer
From page 37

This play is not specifically covered in the official rules. In such a situation the umpires look to Rule 9.01(c), which states: "Each umpire has authority to rule on any point not specifically covered in these rules."

Umpires are instructed to use common sense and fair play in such cases. The umpire crew discussed the play and felt that Rule 7.05(f) was similar in intent. That rule states in part that all runners, including the batter-runner, are awarded two bases if a fair ball sticks in the fence, scoreboard, or shrubbery. Therefore, the crew awarded Damon second base.

Player Identification Answers   *From page 38*

1. Through the 2009 season, Bob Feller is the only pitcher to toss a no-hitter on Opening Day.

2. Eddie Collins is the only player with 3,000 or more hits and fewer than 50 career homers. He retired with 3,315 hits and 47 home runs.

3. Reds' outfielder Cesar Geronimo was the 3,000th strikeout victim for both Bob Gibson in 1974 and Nolan Ryan in 1980.

4. Derek Jeter holds the record for most hits collected in a career at old Yankee Stadium with 1,274.

5. Bill Madlock is the only player with as many as four batting titles (1975–1976, 1981, 1983) who is not in the Hall of Fame.

6. Hall of Famer Tris Speaker is the all-time record holder in doubles with 792.

7. On August 7, 1999, Wade Boggs of Tampa Bay became the first player to collect career hit No. 3,000 with a home run.

8. Vince Coleman is the only player to steal 100 or more bases in a season three years in succession (1985–1987 with St. Louis).

9. Orioles pitcher Jim Palmer won 20 or more games in a season eight times between 1970 and 1978.

10. Rogers Hornsby is the only other player besides Ty Cobb to hit .400 in consecutive seasons since 1900. Cobb did it 1911–1912 with the Tigers and Hornsby in 1924–1925 with the Cardinals.

11. Roger Clemens is the only pitcher to strike out 20 batters in a game twice—April 29, 1986, against the Mariners, and September 18, 1996, against the Tigers.

12. Joe McCarthy is the only manager with 2,000 or more career victories to his credit who has a winning percentage above .600.

Puzzle Solution from page 39

McCarthy was 2,125-1,333 during his managerial days for a .615 winning percentage.

13. George Brett won A.L. batting titles in 1976, 1980, and 1990.

14. Hall of Famer Walter Johnson is the only pitcher in baseball history with 100 or more career shutouts (110).

15. First baseman Mark Grace led all major league batters during the 1990s in hits (1,754) and doubles (364).

Name That Hall of Famer Answers
From page 40

A. Bruce Sutter. Despite a lifetime won-lost record of 68-71, the Hall of Fame reliever made his mark in the majors with 300 career saves and a 2.83 ERA achieved with a devastating split-fingered fastball.

B. Carl Yastrzemski. Yaz is the only player in baseball history to win three batting titles and collect more than 3,000 career hits while posting a lifetime batting average below .300. He won A.L. hitting crowns in 1963, 1967, and 1968, totaled 3,419 hits, and finished with a .285 career BA.

ANSWERS TO QUIZ 10 *From page 41*

1. Besides Ichiro Suzuki in 2001, Tony Oliva is the only other rookie to win a league batting title. He did it in 1965 for the Minnesota Twins.

2. Vince Coleman set a rookie record in 1985 with 110 stolen bases for the St. Louis Cardinals. Tim Raines stole 71 in his rookie season for the Expos in 1981, Rickey Henderson swiped 33 in his first year with the A's in 1979, and Eric Davis had 10 steals in his 1984 rookie campaign with the Reds.

3. With 49 home runs in 1987, Mark McGwire broke the A.L. record for home runs by a rookie set by Al Rosen in 1950 when he hit 37 for the Cleveland Indians.

4. In 1987, Benito Santiago of the Padres set a rookie mark for the longest consecutive-game hitting streak with 34. Santiago's streak lasted from August 25 to October 2.

5. Mariners' pitcher Kazuhiro Sasaki set a major league record for saves in a season with 37 in 2000.

6. In 2001, Albert Pujols of the Cardinals established the National League rookie record for RBI with 130, breaking the old mark of 119 set in 1930 by Wally Berger of the Boston Braves.

7. Despite going 17-10 with a 3.40 ERA and a league-leading 204 strikeouts, Mark Langston finished second in American League Rookie of the Year voting to Seattle Mariners teammate Alvin Davis who hit .284 with 27 homers and 116 RBI.

8. Following is the list of 14 players who collected 200 or more hits during their first season in the major leagues:

Year	Player, Team	H
2001	Ichiro Suzuki, Mariners	242
1927	Lloyd Warner, Pirates	223
1964	Tony Oliva, Twins	217
1929	Dale Alexander, Tigers	215
1929	Johnny Frederick, Dodgers	209
1953	Harvey Kuenn, Tigers	209
1997	Nomar Garciaparra, Red Sox	209
1987	Kevin Seitzer, Royals	207
1934	Hal Trosky, Indians	206
1936	Joe DiMaggio, Yankees	206
1942	Johnny Pesky, Red Sox	205
1929	Roy Johnson, Tigers	201
1964	Dick Allen, Phillies	201
1943	Dick Wakefield, Tigers	200

9. Through 2009, the last rookie pitcher to toss a no-hitter in the majors was right-hander Clay Buchholz of the Boston Red Sox. He held the Baltimore Orioles hitless through nine innings in his second major league appearance on September 1, 2007.

10. Besides Dodgers relief pitcher Larry Sherry in 1959, the only other rookie to win a World Series MVP Award was Livan Hernandez of the Florida Marlins in 1997. Sherry earned the honor by collecting two saves and two wins against the White Sox in 1959. Hernandez won two games against the Indians in 1997.

Fill in the Blank Answers *From page 42*

• Listed are the four players who have won a league Rookie of the Year Award with one team and the MVP Award with another club.

Player	Rookie Team	MVP Team(s)
Frank Robinson	Reds (1956)	Reds (1961)
		Orioles (1966)
Orlando Cepeda	Giants (1958)	Cardinals (1967)
Dick Allen	Phillies (1964)	White Sox (1972)
Andre Dawson	Expos (1977)	Cubs (1987)

• Through 2009 and excluding pitchers who won the Cy Young and the MVP Award in the same season, here are the 18 occurrences when the Cy Young winner and MVP recipient came from the same team.

Year	Team	MVP	Cy Young
1957	Mil. Braves	Hank Aaron	Warren Spahn
1959	White Sox	Nellie Fox	Early Wynn
1960	Pirates	Dick Groat	Vern Law
1961	Yankees	Roger Maris	Whitey Ford
1962	Dodgers	Maury Wills	Don Drysdale
1967	Red Sox	Carl Yastrzemski	Jim Lonborg
1974	Dodgers	Steve Garvey	Mike Marshall
1980	Phillies	Mike Schmidt	Steve Carlton
1982	Brewers	Robin Yount	Pete Vuckovich
1984	Cubs	Ryne Sandberg	Rick Sutcliffe
1988	Dodgers	Kirk Gibson	Orel Hershiser
1990	A's	Rickey Henderson	Bob Welch

Year	Team	MVP	Cy Young
1990	Pirates	Barry Bonds	Doug Drabek
1991	Braves	Terry Pendleton	Tom Glavine
1993	White Sox	Frank Thomas	Jack McDowell
2002	A's	Miguel Tejada	Barry Zito
2005	Cardinals	Albert Pujols	Chris Carpenter
2006	Twins	Justin Morneau	Johan Santana

Name the Players Answers
From page 44

Through the 2009 season, the two active players who have won a league home run crown, RBI title, and batting championship, but not in the same season, are Manny Ramirez and Alex Rodriguez. Ramirez won a HR crown in 2004 and batting title in 2002 with the Red Sox, and an RBI championship in 1999 with the Indians. Rodriguez won a batting crown with the Mariners in 1996, an RBI title in 2002 with the Rangers and in 2007 with the Yankees, and led the A.L. in homers in 2001–2003 with Texas and 2005 and 2007 with New York.

Puzzle Solution from page 43

ANSWERS TO BASEBALL BY THE RULES 5
From page 45

1. False. Lewis should be called out for passing Sandoval between second and third. Sandoval is placed on third base and Lewis credited with a double. Rule 7.08 (h) declares a runner (Lewis) out for passing a preceding runner (Sandoval) before such runner is out.

2. True. According to Rule 6.05(a), the batter is out since the fielder made a legal catch, but because he fell into an out-of-play area, the ball is declared dead and the runners advance one base.

3. True. Rule 7.06: The obstructed runner shall be awarded at least one base beyond the base he had last legally touched before the obstruction. Any preceding runners, forced to advance by the award of bases as the penalty for obstruction, shall advance without liability to be put out.

4. True. DeJesus is out on strikes, and Getz should be called out on his attempted steal due to the interference of DeJesus preventing catcher Lou Marson from making a play.

5. False. According to Rule 4.12(a), a game shall become a suspended game that must be completed at a future date if the game is terminated due to weather if a regulation game is called while an inning is in progress and before the inning is completed, and the visiting team has scored one or more runs to take the lead, and the home team has not retaken the lead.

6. True. According to Rule 4.08, when the occupants of a player's bench show violent disapproval of an umpire's decision, the umpire shall first give warning that such disapproval shall cease. If such action continues, the umpire shall order the offenders from the bench to the clubhouse. If he is unable to detect the offender, or offenders, he may clear the bench of all substitute players. The manager of the offending team shall have the privilege of recalling to the playing field only those players needed for substitution in the game.

7. False. Reynolds should be awarded a home run since the ball deflected off Hawpe's glove and over the outfield wall in fair territory without hitting the ground or the wall.

8. False. In the case where a batter swings and the pitch hits him anyway, the ball is dead and a strike is called.

9. True. Rule 7.09: It is interference by a batter or runner when a fair ball touches him in fair territory before touching a fielder. As long as the fielder had a chance to make a play on the ball, in the umpire's judgment, the runner shall be declared out if a batted ball hits him in fair territory.

10. False. Rule 7.05(c) states, "Each runner including the batter- runner may, without liability to be put out, advance three bases if a fielder deliberately throws his glove at and touches a fair ball. The ball is in play and the batter may advance to home base at his peril." Since Gardner's glove did not touch the ball, the play proceeds as it otherwise would have had the glove not been thrown (no penalty to the defense).

You Make the Call Answer
From page 46

In this situation, Ichiro Suzuki is ruled out, and the ball is dead.

ANSWERS TO QUIZ 11 *From page 47*

1. The four players to put together a hitting streak of 40 or more games since 1900 are Joe DiMaggio (56 in 1941), Pete Rose (44 in 1978), George Sisler (41 in 1922), and Ty Cobb (40 in 1911).

2. Steve Garvey holds the National League record for most consecutive games played with 1,207, with the Dodgers and Padres from September 3, 1975, through July 29, 1983.

3. Shortstop Miguel Tejada is the only active player to sustain a streak of 1,000 or more consecutive games played. He has 1,152 from June 1, 2000, to June 21, 2007, with the A's, Orioles, and Astros.

4. Cubs first baseman Ray Grimes holds the record for most consecutive games with an RBI—17, from June 27 through July 23, 1922. During that span he drove in 27 runs and for the season totaled 99.

5. Ted Williams set the record for reaching base in 84 straight games in 1949 from July 1 through September 27, posting a .518 on-base percentage during that span.

6. Tigers outfielder Roy Cullenbine established the major league record for most consecutive games with a base on balls with 22, from July 2 through July 22, 1947. In this his final year in the majors, he drew a career-high 137 walks.

7. Mark Buehrle of the White Sox holds the mark for most consecutive perfect innings pitched with 15, starting with one-third of an inning on July 18, 2009, a perfect game on July 23, and 5.1 innings on July 28.

8. From May 14 through June 4, 1968, Don Drysdale set a major league record by completing six consecutive shut-outs for the Dodgers.

9. In 1999, Pedro Martinez of the Red Sox set a record for most consecutive games with 10 or more strikeouts with eight, from August 19 through September 27. During that streak he fanned 107 batters and walked only eight.

10. The three players through 2009 to hit a home run in eight straight games are Dale Long, Pirates (1956), Don Mattingly, Yankees (1987), and Ken Griffey, Jr., Mariners (1993).

Name the Manager Answers *From on page 48*

A. The managers for the 20 World Series sweeps through 2009 include: Frank Chance (1907 Cubs), George Stallings (1914 Braves), John McGraw (1922 Giants), Miller Huggins (1927–1928 Yankees), Joe McCarthy (1932, 1938, 1939 Yankees), Casey Stengel (1950 Yankees), Leo Durocher (1954 Giants), Walter Alston (1963 Dodgers), Hank Bauer (1966 Orioles), Sparky Anderson (1976 Reds), Tony La Russa (1989 A's), Lou Piniella (1990 Reds), Joe Torre (1998–1999 Yankees), Terry Francona (2004, 2007 Red Sox), and Ozzie Guillen (2005 White Sox).

B. The five teams Billy Martin managed during his career are the Detroit Tigers, Minnesota Twins, Texas Rangers, New York Yankees, and Oakland A's.

C. Hank Bauer.

ANSWERS TO PHOTO QUIZ 3

From page 49

1. Players who hit four homers in one game:

A. Lou Gehrig	F. Chuck Klein	K. Gil Hodges
B. Rocky Colavito	G. Carlos Delgado	L. Mark Whiten
C. Mike Cameron	H. Shawn Green	M. Willie Mays
D. Pat Seerey	I. Bob Horner	
E. Mike Schmidt	J. Joe Adcock	

2. Former Cy Young Award Winner: John Smoltz

3. Six players who had a 50-homer season:

I. Hank Greenberg	III. Cecil Fielder	V. Roger Maris
II. Mickey Mantle	IV. Luis Gonzalez	VI. Ken Griffey, Jr.

DID YOU KNOW . . . that among the 25 players who have hit 500 or more career home runs, Eddie Murray is the only member not to have a season of 40 or more homers?

During his 21-year career in the majors, Murray hit 504 lifetime homers with a single-season high of 33 in 1983 with the Baltimore Orioles.

ANSWERS TO QUIZ 12 *From page 50*

1. The two players to hit two pinch-hit home runs in one World Series are Chuck Essegian of the Dodgers in 1959 and Bernie Carbo of the Red Sox in 1975.

2. The 12 Yankees to win World Series MVP honors since 1955 are Don Larsen (1956), Bob Turley (1958), Bobby Richardson (1960), Whitey Ford (1961), Ralph Terry (1962), Reggie Jackson (1977), Bucky Dent (1978), John Wetteland (1996), Scott Brosius (1998), Mariano Rivera (1999), Derek Jeter (2000), and Hideki Matsui (2009).

3. The only player to collect 10 hits in a World Series with different teams is Paul Molitor—with the Brewers in 1982 and the Blue Jays in 1993.

4. In 1965, Sandy Koufax of the Dodgers pitched a perfect game against the Cubs on September 9, and later picked up two victories in the World Series against the Twins.

5. Matt Williams is the only player, through 2009, to hit a World Series home run with three different teams. He did it with the Giants in 1989, the Indians in 1997, and the Diamondbacks in 2001.

6. The 14 walk-off home runs in World Series play through 2009 include: Tommy Henrich, Yankees (1949, Game 1); Dusty Rhodes, Giants (1954, Game 1); Eddie Mathews, Braves (1957, Game 4); Bill Mazeroski, Pirates (1960, Game 7); Mickey Mantle, Yankees (1964, Game 3); Carlton Fisk, Red Sox (1975, Game 6); Kirk Gibson, Dodgers (1988, Game 1); Mark McGwire, A's (1988, Game 3); Kirby Puckett, Twins (1991, Game 6); Joe Carter, Blue Jays (1993, Game 6); Chad Curtis, Yankees (1999, Game 3); Derek Jeter, Yankees (2001, Game 4); Alex Gonzalez, Marlins (2003, Game 4); and Scott Podsednik, White Sox (2005, Game 2).

7. Bob Gibson is the only pitcher in baseball history to have two World Series Game 7 complete-game victories, accomplishing the feat with the Cardinals in 1964 against the Yankees and in 1967 against the Red Sox.

8. In 1928, Babe Ruth set a record for most hits in a four-game World Series with 10 against the St. Louis Cardinals.

9. Moe Drabowski is the only relief pitcher to strike out 10 or more batters in a World Series game. He worked 6.2 innings in relief in Game 1 of the

**Puzzle Solution
from page 51**

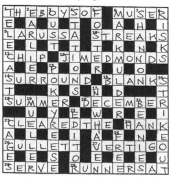

1966 World Series for the Orioles and fanned 11 Dodger batters.

10. With three home runs off CC Sabathia in the 2009 World Series, Chase Utley of the Phillies became the second batter to hit three homers off the same pitcher in one Fall Classic matchup, equaling the mark set by Yogi Berra of the Yankees who homered three times off Dodgers pitcher Don Newcombe in the 1956 World Series.

Team Identification Answers
From page 52

A. Through 2009, the five players who put together a 200-hit season in both leagues include George Sisler (St. Louis Browns, Boston Braves), Al Oliver (Texas Rangers, Montreal Expos), Bill Buckner (Chicago Cubs, Boston Red Sox), Steve Sax (Los Angeles Dodgers, New York Yankees), and Vladimir Guerrero (Anaheim Angels, Montreal Expos).

B. The five players since 1900 and through 2009 who won batting titles with two different teams are Nap Lajoie (A's, Indians), Rogers Hornsby (Cardinals, Braves), Lefty O'Doul (Phillies, Dodgers), Jimmie Foxx (A's, Red Sox), and Bill Madlock (Cubs, Pirates).

ANSWERS TO QUIZ 13 *From page 53*

1. The six players to win a league MVP, batting title, and Gold Glove in the same season are Carl Yastrzemski (1967), Dave Parker (1978), Keith Hernandez (1979), Willie McGee (1985), Ichiro Suzuki (2001), and Joe Mauer (2009).

2. Besides Hanley Ramirez, the 12 other players to win a Rookie of the Year Award and a batting title during their careers are Jackie Robinson, Willie Mays, Harvey Kuenn, Frank Robinson, Billy Williams, Pete Rose, Tony Oliva, Rod

Carew, Fred Lynn, Nomar Garciaparra, Ichiro Suzuki, and Albert Pujols.

3. In 2006, Joe Girardi won the N.L. Manager of the Year Award with Florida, a team that finished with a 78-84 record.

4. Lance Berkman holds the record for most extra base hits in a season (94) for switch-hitters, set in 2001 with the Astros.

5. Besides Addie Joss, the five other multiple no-hit pitchers to have a perfect game to their credit are Sandy Koufax, Mark Buehrle, Randy Johnson, Jim Bunning, and Cy Young.

6. Alex Rodriguez (2), Ryan Howard (3), and David Ortiz (2) are the three active players with multiple RBI titles through 2009.

7. Don Sutton never led the league in strikeouts despite finishing his career with 3,574, seventh on the all-time list.

8. Beside Gary Sheffield, Fred McGriff is the only other player to hit 30 or more homers in a season with five different teams. Sheffield did it for the Padres, Marlins, Braves, Dodgers, and Yankees. McGriff did it for the Blue Jays, Padres, Braves, Rays, and Cubs.

9. Dave Winfield is the only player to collect his 3,000th career hit off a future Hall of Famer: he reached his historic plateau against Dennis Eckersley on September 16, 1993.

10. Vince Coleman is the only player to steal 100 bases in a season without hitting a home run when he swiped 109 bases in 1986 without a homer.

ANSWERS TO BASEBALL BY THE RULES 6 *From page 54*

1. Fair. 2. Fair. 3. Foul. 4. Fair. 5. Foul. 6. Fair. 7. Fair. 8. Fair. 9. Foul. 10. Fair.

You Make the Call Answer

From page 55

Both Garrett Jones and Ryan Doumit score, and Andrew McCutchen moves to second. On this play, each runner is entitled to advance two bases beyond the base he held when the wild throw was made. McCutchen gets only second because he had not yet reached first when the overthrow occurred.

ANSWERS TO QUIZ 14   *From page 56*

1. The four Red Sox batters to win consecutive batting titles are Ted Williams, Carl Yastrzemski, Wade Boggs, and Nomar Garciaparra.

2. The last pitcher to have consecutive 25-win seasons is Sandy Koufax in 1965–1966 with the Dodgers.

3. The three Yankee managers named "Joe" who won World Series titles are Joe McCarthy, Joe Torre, and Joe Girardi.

4. John Smoltz is the only pitcher to lead the league in wins (1996, 2006) and saves (2002) during his career.

5. The four different Reds players to win an MVP Award during the 1970s are Johnny Bench (1970, 1972), Pete Rose (1973), Joe Morgan (1975–1976), and George Foster (1977).

6. Besides Chief Meyers and Joe Mauer, the only other catcher to lead his league in on-base percentage was Mickey Cochrane of the A's in 1933 with a .459 mark.

7. The four players to hit 45-plus homers with 130 RBI in four consecutive seasons are Babe Ruth (1926–1931), Ken Griffey (1996–1999), Sammy Sosa (1998–2001), and Ryan Howard (2006–2009).

8. Joe (1,537) and Dom (618) DiMaggio combined for 2,155 career RBI, second to the total established by brothers Hank and Tommy Aaron.

9. Beside Mark Teixeira, the six other Yankees to lead the A.L. in both homers and RBI in the same season include Babe Ruth, Lou Gehrig, Joe DiMaggio, Mickey Mantle, Roger Maris, and Alex Rodriguez.

10. In 1963, Dave Nicholson of the White Sox was the first player to fan 150-plus times in a season, with a league-leading total of 175.

Name That Player Answers
From page 57

A. Babe Ruth. **B.** Vern Stephens. **C.** Babe Ruth. **D.** Greg Maddux. **E.** Grover Alexander. **F.** Lefty Grove. **G.** Jimmy Rollins, Willie Wilson, Ichiro Suzuki, and Juan Samuel.